MUSIC

INDUSTRY

Connection

resources for:

ARTISTS
PRODUCERS
MANAGERS

by
JAWAR

JaWar has planted a seed in the Atlanta Music Community that is guaranteed to flourish season after season.
I challenge you to find a resource more dedicated to the Atlanta Music Industry.
Coriya Burns, Hot 107.5, Account Executive

This book provides practical information about the business of music and will be an invaluable tool for anyone engaged in the music industry.
Vernon Slaughter, Atlanta Entertainment Attorney

Music Industry Connection is an awesome resource to get your feet wet when approaching the business of music in Atlanta. You can't beat it for a handy look at various facilities and service providers for whatever you need to get done next.
Cha-Cha Jones, DJ & Radio Personality

Through the Atlanta Music Industry Connection, JaWar has provided a valuable resource for independent artists, managers and producers looking to boost their careers to the next level.
Tirrell D. Whittley, Liquid Soul Media & Liquid Soul Radio

The Music Industry Connection is a must for anyone seeking to become a player in the Atlanta Music Market.
Stephen Strother, CEO, ARMUSIC1.com

ISBN: 0-9759380-0-2
Library of Congress Control Number 2004096435

by JaWar

FIRST EDITION

Published by

Music Industry Connection, LLC
P.O. Box 52682, Atlanta, GA 30355, USA
800-963-0949 www.mt101.com questions@mt101.com

Printed in the U.S.A.

The information provided in this book is intended only as a resource guide for aspiring artists, producers, engineers and managers in the music industry. Remember to always verify the company and contact names found in this book before submitting material. There are a number of resources needed to achieve success in the business of music that are not contained in this book. The authors and publishers have attempted to verify the accuracy of the resources in this book; however, the information provided is subject to change. The authors and publisher disclaim all responsibility for any loss or damages.

Cover Design: Derrick Leslie of Next Level Entertainment
Edited by Seneferu Ast
Interview transcribed by Candice Monique Butler

The goal of the author is to provide a how to resource tool, reference guide and directory for artists, producers, managers and other music industry professionals involved in the Growing Atlanta Music Industry and to increase awareness for businesses engaged in the Atlanta Music Industry Dynamic.

In addition, the book is designed to give aspiring artists, producers and managers practical steps and tips for achieving their goals and realizing their success. Some of the information is repeated in the book because we thought it was important to that aspiring music industry professional. For instance, the recording studios are listed in both the artists and producer sections.

ACKNOWLEDGEMENTS

Writing and publishing the Atlanta Music Industry Connection Book has been a tremendous learning experience. The first printing of this book would not have been possible without the support of family, friends and business associates listed below. Thank you for helping me achieve my goal and realize my potential. Shem Hotep!
JaWar

Queston Tasby-Industry Status Magazine, Natasha Brison, Esq., Kirk D. Woods-Heavy Hittaz Productions, Mona "Mother of Civilization" Fenderson, Bonyetta Brison, Hasson S. Diggs, Dior Metcalf, Anquinette Dasina Williams, DJ Knotts-Black Trump Entertainment, Gene Black and Willie Bell Chatmon.

TABLE OF CONTENTS

ARTIST DEVELOPMENT

- Copyrights 9
- Trademarks 10
- Performance Rights Organizations 10
- Recording Studios 11
- Where may I get a barcode? 14
- CD/DVD/Vinyl Manufacturers 15
- Printers for flyers & CD Inserts 16
- Distribution Companies 17
- Photographers 19
- Music Conferences 21
- How do I find more shows to perform in? 22
- Record Companies 26
- How to Market Your Independent Release 30
- When do I need a manager? 33
- When do I need an attorney? 34
- Artist's Revenue Stream 35

PRODUCER'S WORKSHOP

- What equipment do I need? 37
- How do I insure my equipment? 37
- When do I need an entertainment attorney? 38
- Copyrights 39
- Trademarks 39
- Performance Rights Organizations 40
- Recording Studios 40
- Recording Music Retail Stores 44
- CD/DVD/Vinyl Manufacturers 46
- Printers for flyers & CD Inserts 47
- Music Conferences 48
- Mastering Facilities 49
- Music Producers 50
- How should a producer market their tracks? 55

➢ Producer's Revenue Stream 55

MANAGER'S CORNER

➢ What skills do I need as a manager? 59
➢ What are the three types of managers? 59
➢ When do I need an entertainment attorney? 60
➢ Who pays the manager? 60
➢ Management Organizations 61
➢ Management Companies 61
➢ Management Books 64
➢ Interview with Dayo & Al of Own Music 67
➢ Manager's Revenue Stream 77

INFORMATION FOR ALL

➢ When do I need a business license or tax I.D.? 79
➢ How do I get a business license? 79
➢ What is a tax I.D.? 80
➢ How do I get a tax I.D.? 80
➢ What is the difference between a business license and a tax I.D.? 80
➢ Where may I get business cards for free? 80
➢ How may I get flyers printed for free? 81
➢ How may I get 50 to 100 promotional CDs free? 81
➢ Where may I use the Internet for free? 82
➢ What is a One-Sheet? 82
➢ What is a Split-Sheet? 83
➢ What is Soundexchange? 83
➢ Music Retail Stores 84
➢ Radio Stations 90
➢ Music Magazines 93
➢ Using Record Pools to Test-Market Your Next Hit 96
➢ How are CD sales tracked? 99
➢ How do I ensure proper credit for my

CD sales? 99
- Does SoundScan also track CDs sold at live performances? 99
- Who tracks and monitors radio airplay? 99
- Promoters 100
- Music Business Books 102
- Internet Resource Guide 103
- Graphic Design Companies 103
- Music Consultants 105
- Music Organizations 106
- Entertainment Attorneys 108
- Video Production Companies 113
- Atlanta Venues & Clubs 116
- Creating Wealth 119

ARTIST DEVELOPMENT

What Copyright Forms are needed to protect my music?

You will need copyright Form PA & Form SR.

Obtain copyright forms through:

- Library of Congress, Copyright Office, Register of Copyrights, 101 Independence Avenue, S.E., Washington, D.C. 20559-6000
  Phone: 202-707-3000
  lcweb.loc.gov

- Copyright Order Form Hotline
  (202) 707-9100

How much does it cost to register a copyright with the U.S. Library of Congress?

When this book was printed it cost $30 to register a copyright. You may copyright a collection of songs under one title for $30 as long as the author of all the songs is the same.

Order a Copyright Kit from Gordon Publishing Company

- P) 678-698-7776
  www.copyrightkit.com

How do I protect my band name and logo in Georgia?

Apply for a trademark with the Georgia Secretary of State.

How do I contact the Georgia Secretary of State?

- Office of Secretary of State Corporation Division,
  Suite 315, West Tower, 2 MLK Dr., Atlanta, GA 30334
  P) 404-656-2861 F) 404-657-6380
  www.sos.state.ga.us

How do I protect my band name and logo in the United States?

To protect an artist stage name, a band's name and/or logo apply for a trademark or servicemark through the U.S. Patent & Trademark Office.

- U.S. Patent and Trademark Office
  General Information Services Division
  Crystal Plaza 3, RM 2 C02
  Washington, D.C. 20231
  800-786-9199
  www.uspto.gov

What is a PRO (Performing Rights Organization)?

A PRO is an organization responsible for collecting & distributing performance royalties (money) to songwriters and music publishers.

How do I contact a PRO?

- ASCAP-American Society of Composers,
  Authors and Publishers

541 Tenth St. NW, #PMB 500, Atlanta, GA 30318
P) 404-351-1224 F) 404-351-1252
www.ascap.com

- BMI-Broadcast Music, Inc.
  P.O. Box 19199, Atlanta, GA 31126
  P) 404-261-5151
  www.bmi.com

- SESAC
  55 Music Square East, Nashville, TN 37203
  P) 615-320-0055
  www.sesac.com

RECORDING STUDIOS

An artist or producer should determine the goal, create a practical plan and rehearse the plan before paying studio costs to record. This will save a great deal of time and money.

There is a wide range of studios at your disposal. When it comes to recording, a good rule of thumb is the fewer the surprises, the better off you are. With that in mind, one of the questions you will want to ask is if the quoted price includes the studio engineer's fee, as sometimes it does and sometimes it doesn't, so remember to ask. In addition, many studios offer block (discount) rates when you book (reserve) say 10 or more hours at a time. Therefore, it is to your advantage to block out studio time to save money. However, if you are not accustomed to recording for 10 hours then this may be a waste of time and money. Studio prices can range from $25/hr to $150/hr. Remember to bring your own CD-Rs and other record-able devices to the studio. The studio will probably have some on hand, but it will cost you a lot more to by it from the studio than to bring you own. You should remember, that the recording studio is a business, so they are going to make every penny they can. In addition, to studio cost you want to ask about the experience of the studio engineer that will work on your project and the style of music the studio normally records. Ideally, you also want to ensure that there is chemistry between you and the engineer. In summary, a few factors to consider before choosing a studio are: **studio cost, experience of studio engineer, whether the engineer records your style of music often and chemistry between artist, producer & studio engineer.** Below is a list of Recording Studios.

- 1210 Recording Studios
  1210 Spring Street, Atlanta, GA 30309
  P) 404-347-8998

- 500 Grand Studios
  Contact: Carlos Foreman
  1850 Graves Rd., Suite 215, Norcross, GA 30093
  P) 678-969-9121

- Big Cat Studios
  Contact: Tarina
  500 Bishop St., Suite E5, Atlanta, GA 30318
  P) 404-603-8229 P) 404-641-7210

- Blackberry Recording Studios
  3141 East Ponce De Leon, Scottsdale, GA 30079
  P) 404-687-0920

- Capstone Musicworks
  Contact: Stacey Wallace
  8385 Cherokee Blvd. Suite 200, Douglasville, GA 30135
  P) 770-947-3534 Cell) 678-698-7956
  www.capstonemusicworks.com
  swallace@capstonemusicworks.com

- Down 4 Life Recording Studios
  5127 Old National Hwy, Atlanta, GA 30349
  P) 404-766-7377

- Electronika Recording Studios
  2963 Stone Road, Atlanta, GA 30344
  P) 404-766-0288

- Evolution Recording Studios
  Contact: Reggie Regg
  3131 Campbelton Rd., Suite-H, Atlanta, GA 30311
  P) 404-840-3846

- Golden Boy Recording Studios
  Contact: Ray Hamilton
  5319 Old National Hwy, College Park, GA 30349
  P) 404-684-5999 F) 404-684-5973

- House 21 Entertainment Recording Studio
  Contact: Mike
  2100 Drake Court, Lithonia, GA 30058
  P) 678-508-3742

- Joi Recording Studios
  2356 Park Central Blvd., Decatur, GA 30035
  P) 678-418-9973

- Lakefront Studios
  Contact: Benjamin Cornthwaite
  P) 770-602-0995 F) 770-602-1206 M) 404-925-5583
  www.lakefrontstudios.com

- Maze Recording Studio
  Contact: Derrick
  2963 Lambert Dr., Atlanta, GA 30324
  Cell) 770-633-5747 P) 678-428-3437

- Paradise Recording Studio
  Contact: James Gray
  1651 Link Overlook, Atlanta, GA 30088
  P) 404-351-0086
  Paradise1651@aol.com

- Patchwerk Recording Studios
  1094 Hemphill, Atlanta, GA 30318
  P) 404-874-9880

- Reel to Reel Recording Studios
  1440 Dutch Valley Place, Suite 790, Atlanta, GA 30324
  P) 404-817-3883

Where may I get a barcode?

- U.C.C. – Uniform Code Council
  Customer Service 7887
  Washington Village Dr., Suite 300
  Dayton, OH 45459
  P) 937-435-3870 F) 937-435-7317
  www.uc-council.org
  info@uc-council.org

How do I get a parental advisory label for my CDs?

The industry standard parental advisory label that is placed on CDs may be obtained through the RIAA.

How do I contact the RIAA?

- RIAA (Recording Industry Association of America)

1330 Connecticut Avenue, Suite 300
Washington D.C. 20036
P) 202-775-0101 F) 202-775-7253
www.riaa.com
webmaster@riaa.com

CD/DVD/VINYL MANUFACTURERS

- A Black Clan Distribution & Manufacturing Inc.
  Contact: Juan C. Williams
  P) 877-706-7316 P) 770-907-8665 F) 770-907-9216
  www.ablackclan.com
  juan@ablackclan.com

- Atlanta Manufacturing Group
  83 Walton St., Third Floor, Atlanta, GA 30303
  P) 404-230-9559 F) 230-9558
  www.amgcds.com
  info@amgcds.com

- Creative Media
  2783 Senecca Trail, Duluth, GA 30096-6298
  P) 770-447-8137
  www.creativemedia.com
  sales@creativemedia.com

- MDS
  824-B Memorial Dr., Atlanta, GA 30316
  P) 404-584-0372 F) 404-584-9406
  www.mdsinconline.com

- Mindzai
  1139 Euclid Avenue, Atlanta, GA 30307
  P) 404-577-8484 F) 404-577-5895
  www.mindzai.net

- ON4 Productions
  684 Antone St., NW Suite 110, Atlanta, GA 30318
  P) 888-710-5157 P) 404-603-9900 F) 404-351-7775
  www.on4prod.com

- Project 70 Audio Services
  433 Bishop St., NW Suite CD, Atlanta, GA 30310
  P) 404-875-7000 F) 404-875-7007
  www.project70.com

- Straight from the Soul
  5741 Wells Circle, Stone Mountain, GA 30087
  P) 770-413-2464
  straightent@aol.com

- Tape Warehouse
  2688 Peachtree Sq., Doraville, GA 30360
  P) 770-458-1679 F) 770-458-0276
  www.tapewarehouse.com

- Yourmusiconcd.com
  Contact: Suwat
  421 A-1 Pike Blvd., Lawrenceville, GA 30045
  P) 877-442-0933 P) 678-442-0933 F) 678-377-9765
  sns@yourmusiconcd.com

PRINTERS FOR FLYERS & CD-INSERTS

- Ananse Creative
  Contact: Salah Ananse
  P) 404-344-9343 P) 678-592-4795
  www.anansecreative.com
  anansecreative@bellsouth.net

- Digiprint
  2395 Pleasantdale Rd., Suite 4-B, Atlanta, GA 30340
  P) 770-368-2060 F) 770-368-9943

- Extreme Media
  1440 Dutch Valley Pl., Suite 160
  P) 404-815-0553 F) 404-815-0314
  www.extremeatlanta.com

- Identity Graphics & Printing
  Contact: Ira Watkins
  254 E. Paces Ferry Rd., Atlanta, GA 30305
  P) 404-417-9777
  www.identitypress.net

- Small Business Promotions, Inc.
  P.O. Box 1348, Lithonia, GA 30058
  P) 678-886-8792 P) 770-557-0938
  www.designsnprint.com
  orders@designsnprint.com

- Star Shooters
  277-B East Paces Ferry Rd, Atlanta, GA 30305
  P) 404-869-8844 F) 404-869-8833

- Southern Poster Printing
  3862 Stevens Ct., Tucker, GA
  P) 888-872-8194 P) 404-872-8194

- Southern Stamp & Stencil
  428 Edgewood Ave., Atlanta, GA 30312
  P) 800-241-0985 P) 404-522-4431
  www.southernstamp.com
  info@southernstamp.com

DIGITAL DISTRIBUTION COMPANIES

- www.101distribution.com
- www.buyindiemusic.com
- www.buythiscd.com
- www.cdbaby.com

- www.cdfreedom.com
- www.cdpimp.com
- www.cdstreet.com
- www.galaxydiscs.com
- www.indiegate.com
- www.indypendence.com
- www.lightningcd.com
- www.musicfist.com
- www.rapstation.com
- www.soundclick.com
- www.theorchard.com

DISTRIBUTION COMPANIES

- IMD-International Music Distribution
  Contact: Brad McDonald
  764 Glenshire Ct., Riverdale, GA 30274
  P) 770-909-7427 F) 770-909-7756
  bradimd@bellsouth.net

- Red Distribution
  2531 Briarcliff Rd., NE, Atlanta, GA
  www.redmusic.com
  P) 404-679-6084

- Select-O-Hits Distribution
  Contact: New Music Buyer
  1981 Fletcher Creek Dr., Memphis, TN 38133
  P) 901-388-1190
  www.selectohits.com

- Southern Music Distribution
  P.O. Box 921969, Atlanta, GA 30010
  P) 770-447-5159
  www.southernmusicdigital.com

Websites that sell domain names or website address.

- www.buydomains.com
- www.networksolutions.com
- www.omnis.com

PHOTOGRAPHERS

- D'Cals Photography
  P) 404-379-8769

- D2K Models Design Group
  1016 Howell Mill Rd., Suite 1210, Atlanta, GA 30318
  P) 404-441-5794
  www.d2kmodels.com
  moussa@d2kmodels.com

- Keith Morgan
  P) 770-994-0395

- Kenny's Photography
  Contact: Kenneth L. Hawkins Jr.
  1729 Rogers Ave. SW, Atlanta, GA 30310
  P) 404-758-7301 Cell) 404-247-2018

- Laser Photographics
  Contact: Christi
  290 Hilderbrand Dr., Suite B-9, Atlanta, GA 30328
  P) 404-531-0555 F) 404-531-0044
  www.laserphotographics.com
  laserphotgraphics@mindsping.com

- Photomax
  Contact: C.G.
  3375 Buford Hwy, Suite 1020, Atlanta, GA 30329
  P) 404-320-1494 F) 404-320-6291
  www.photomax1hr.com

photomax@aol.com

- Primetime
  Contact: Omar M. Cherif
  P.O. Box 49531, Atlanta, GA 30359
  P) 404-731-2343
  www.primetimeatlanta.com

- Robin Henson Photograph
  P) 404-377-5062
  Robin.pix@mindspring.com

- Sean Cokes
  Hilliard St., NE, Studio 14, Atlanta, GA 30312
  P) 404-524-4821

- Studio 305 Photography
  P) 678-495-2339 P) 678-760-6561
  studio305ent@aol.com
  cornellmcbride@yahoo.com

- Holidayshots Photography
  Contact: Tharwat Abdul-Malik
  3535 Peachtree Rd., Suite 520-151, Atlanta, GA 30326
  P) 404-518-0990
  www.holidayshots.com
  photographer@holidayshots.com

- Top Notch Photo
  Contact: David Yates
  P) 678-984-5847
  www.topnotchphoto.com

- Visual Science Photography
  Contact: Tyson Franklin
  P) 678-464-2149

MUSIC CONFERENCES

Music conferences are a fantastic way to network, negotiate and know the business of music. By attending a music conference you have the ability to create windows of opportunity for yourself. This is achieved by having a clearly identifiable goal. For instance, your goal may be to network with a Kemetic Records Representative or to gather contact information from other industry professionals. Music conferences may also be used to negotiate deals. For example, a conference may be a great time to discuss in greater detail a project that you are working on with another industry professional. To make the best of your time, contact the person you intend on meeting with prior to the conference, set an itinerary, a time to meet and a location. This ensures that you both know what to expect from the meeting and that time is scheduled to accomplish the task. With practical planning you will find that music conferences are a fantastic way to network, negotiate and know the business of music. Below is a list of music conferences to consider attending:.

- A&R Music1.com, LLC.
  Contact: Stephen Strother
  2132 Sara Ashley Way, Suite 300 Lithonia, GA 30058
  P) 770-686-9100
  www.armusic1.com

- Atlantis Music Conference
  1339 Canton Rd., Suite E, Marietta, GA 30066
  P) 770-499-8600 F) 770-499-8650
  www.atlantismusic.com

- Dynamic Producer
  www.dynamicproducer.com
  info@dynamicproducer.com

- Million Dollar Record Pool Conference
  2459 Roosevelt Hwy. Suite B-1, College Park GA 30337
  P) 404-766-1275 F) 404.559.0117
  http://mildol.com/
  mde@mildol.com

- **MUSIC THERAPY 101**
  P.O. Box 52682, Atlanta, GA 30355
  800-963-0949
  www.mt101.com
  questions@mt101.com

- Southeast Urban Music Conference (SMI)
  P.O. Box 670296, Marietta, GA 30066
  P) 770-621-5820 F) 770-973-0136
  www.smiurban.com
  smiurban@comcast.net

How do I find more shows to perform in?

Ask other bands/artists where they perform and how they hear about new opportunities. This allows you to benefit from someone else's knowledge very fast. Likewise, you should share your information with other artist.

Networking is your key to success here. What this means is that you want to ask everyone that you know related to the music industry if they are aware of places where you may perform. For example, ask folks that work at music retail stores, studio engineers, party/club promoters, DJs, music publicists, booking agents, record company executives and entertainment attorneys. Letting the right people know you are ready and willing to perform is a step in the right direction to finding more places to showcase your talent. Another way to showcase your talent is to create your own show. Pursue local publications such as Rolling Out Weekly and Creative Loafing Newspapers, as there are often announcements for talent shows and open-mics. Details about creating your own show will be in the next book.

REMEMBER TO:

- Ask other artists where they perform.
- Ask music industry professionals if they know of places for you to perform.
- Read Rolling Out Weekly & Creative Loafing for Talent Showcase Announcements.
- Create your own venue for performing.

TALENT SHOW ORGANIZERS

Performing in front of A&R and other music industry professionals should not be your sole purpose for showcasing your talent on stage. If executed properly, whether you perform in front of 1 person or 1,000 people, you can optimize your live performance experience to improve your craft, increase your fan base, generate sales and above all else have fun!

First, practice, practice, practice before you set foot on stage. This will build your confidence while on stage. Furthermore, you will demonstrate that you are serious about your craft. Second, know that every performance is more mental than physical. So, prepare yourself as though your next performance is in front of loyal fans that have paid hard earned money to see you perform. Third, get someone to video tape all of your performances. This way you can go back and review your show. Keep in mind that other bands, speakers and athletic teams do this to improve their craft. In addition, at some point in your career you may be able to professionally package and sell the footage. Fourth, designate someone to get contact names, physical & email addresses and phone numbers of everyone at your performance. By doing so you can invite those same people to your next performance. When your

CDs and t-shirts are ready you will have a potential client base interested in supporting you. While these steps just touch the surface of using live performances to improve your craft, increase your fan base, generate sales and have fun while on stage this should give you an idea as to how you may best utilize your talent, no matter the size of the audience. Below is a list of companies that produce regular events for artists to showcase their skills and abilities.:

- A&R Hookup
  Contact: Stephen Strother
  2132 Sara Ashley Way, Suite 300 Lithonia, GA 30058
  P) 770-686-9100

- A&J Connection
  Contact: Janice or A.J.
  P) 770-981-5114
  ajsconn@bellsouth.net

- Adonis International
  Contact: Andre Goolsby
  230 Peachtree Center, Suite 56341, Atlanta, GA 30343
  P) 800-796-8619 P) 770-621-2511
  Talent Hotline: 770-621-2567
  www.adonis-international.com
  andreadonisintl@yahoo.com

- Dres Tha Beatnik
  Attn: MIC CLUB
  www.4kingsent.com

- Lady Di/Bar Entertainment
  Contact: Jocelyn D. Vickers
  P) 404-843-4970 F) 770-960-5981
  www.ldbr-entgrp.com

- Mass Appeal Media
  Contact: Angie the Hip Hop Angel
  P) 770-912-5864

- Taylord Entertainment
  Contact: Frank Taylor
  4600 East Ponce De Leon, Suite 406,
  Clarkston, GA 30021
  P) 770-482-8797
  www.tay-lordentertainment.com

RECORD COMPANIES

- Air Gospel
  881 Memorial Drive, SE, Atlanta, GA 30316
  P) 404-524-6835 F) 404-681-0033
  www.airgospel.com
  air@airgospel.com

- Aquemni Records
  Contact: Janet Faison
  684 Anton St. Suite 100, Atlanta, GA 30318
  P) 404-350-3332 P) 404-603-4736
  www.outkast.com

- ArcTheFinger Records
  Contact: Brian Knott
  1372 Peachtree St., Suite 300, Atlanta, GA 30309
  P) 404-339-0051 Ext. 201 F) 404-339-0061
  www.archthefinger.com
  b@archthefinger.com

- Big Cat Records
  500 Bishop St., Suite E5, Atlanta, GA 30318
  P.O. Box 490956, Atlanta, GA 30349
  P) 866-603-8229 F) 404-603-9231
  www.bigcatrecords.net

- Big Oomp Records
  Attn: Store Promotions Dept.
  1079 MLK Drive NW, Ste 2, Atlanta, GA 30314
  P) 404-758-4210
  nakia@bigoomprecords.com

- BME (Black Market Entertainment) Recordings
  Contact: Dwayne "Emperor" Searcy
  2144 Hills Ave., Suite D-2, Atlanta, GA 30318
  P) 404-367-8130 F) 404-367-8630
  www.bmerecordings.com

dsearch@bmerecordings.com

- Break'Em Off Records
  Contact: Dan Brown
  764 Glenshire Ct., Riverdale, GA 30274
  P) 770-994-9003 F) 770-994-9046
  www.breakemoffrecords.com
  brkemoffrec@aol.com

- CGI
  Attn: Platinum Entertainment
  11415 Old Roswell Rd., Alpharetta, GA 30004
  P) 770-664-9262 F) 770-664-7316

- Columbia Records
  Contact: Sharon M. Fitzgerald
  1365 Benning Place, Suite 4, Atlanta, GA 30307
  P) 404-584-8937
  Sharon_Fitzgerald@sonymusic.com

- Deep End Records
  3469 Lawrencville Hwy., Suite 304, Tucker, GA 30084
  P) 678-280-0295 F) 770-908-8798
  www.deepend-records.com

- Def Jam South
  1349 West Peachtree St., #2, Atlanta, GA 30309 or
  P.O. Box 78386, Atlanta, GA 30357
  P) 404-875-6695 P) 404-876-1173
  www.defjamsouth.net

- Fort Knox
  3695 Cascade Rd., #138, Atlanta, GA 30331
  P) 404-862-4426

- Gimptown Records
  P.O. Box 54700, Civic Center Station,
  Atlanta, GA 30308

P) 770-996-9007
www.goldwax.com
goldwax@aol.com

- Hitzone Entertainment
  P) 404-931-1207

- **KEMETIC RECORDS**
  www.mt101.com

- Money Makers Records
  3500 Lenox Rd., Suite 1500, Atlanta, GA 30326
  P) 404-819-7186

- NME Records
  Contact: Kris Fite
  Midtown Proscenium Center
  1170 Peachtree St., Suite 1200, Atlanta, GA 30309
  P) 404-885-5754 F) 404-885-5764
  www.nmerecords.com
  kris_fite@nmerecords.com

- Real Deal Records
  794 Evander Holyfield Hwy, Fairburn, GA 30212
  P) 770-461-5433 F) 770-461-5011

- Real Life Records
  220 Timberland Tr., Riverdale, GA 30274
  P) 770-477-5505

- Rocky Road Records
  2945 Stone Hogan, Suite 103, Atlanta, GA 30331
  P) 404-349-1498

- Selsum Records
  Contact: Tangela Sumra
  401 East Lake Dr., Marietta, GA 30062
  P) 678-560-1067

selsumrecords@aol.com

- Sierre-Pearl Records
  Contact: Pearl Muldrow
  P.O. Box 2417 Jonesboro, GA 30237-2417
  P) 770-703-6655
  www.johnnymo.info
  sierrapearl@comcast.net

- Slam Jamz 2
  7139 Hwy 85, Suite 293, Riverdale, GA 30274
  P) 770-997-9124

- So So Def Records
  685 Lambert Dr., NE, Atlanta, GA 30324-4125
  P) 404-888-9900 F) 404-888-9901

- Stone Legend Music
  Contact: Corey "Da Masta" Wilson
  P) 404-766-6649 F) 770-968-3361 Cell) 678-548-6456

- Sys Records
  P.O. Box 371485, Decatur, GA 30037
  P) 404-259-9943

- Triad Records
  6350 McDonough Dr., Ste A, Norcross, GA 30093
  P) 770-840-0608 F) 70-446-2036

- Trump Tight Records
  P.O. Box 861, Scottsdale, GA 30079
  P) 404-830-3498

- Universal (Records) Studios
  5405 Metric Place, Suite 300, Norcross, GA 30092
  P) 770-849-6107 F) 770-263-8132

- WEA-Warner/Elektra/Atlantic
  Contact: James Rhodes
  817 West Peachtree Street #300, Atlanta, GA 30308
  P) 404-602-3406 F) 404-602-3362
  James.Rhodes@weac.com

- Worldwide Entertainment
  3079 E. Shadowlawn Ave., Atlanta, GA 30305
  P) 404-760-0599

How to Market Your Independent Release

A practical plan, a passion to succeed and a willingness to innovate are most important in marketing your independent release. Make sure your product stands the test of time. In short: your music should be **HOT!**

Make a list of music retail stores, night clubs, colleges & universities, high schools, coffee houses, malls, college, community radio stations, college & high school papers and local magazines. The list of venues and locations should be within an hour of your home market. This will give you the opportunity to penetrate your core market and build a solid fan-base. This is especially, important for the independent label and artist who count on selling CDs, merchandise and tickets to live performances to pay the mortgage.

The next step is to obtain the physical and email addresses, phone and fax numbers of each location mentioned. Begin contacting the colleges and high schools that have newspapers. The goal is to get the music and/or entertainment writer to either interview you and/or write a review of your HOT Music. The writers should receive your type written bio, an 8x10 black & white glossy photo and professionally recorded CD. However, always correspond with the music reviewer before submitting your materials, as some writers may have special requirements. For instance, they may accept a black & white 4x6 photo versus an 8x10 black & white glossy. In addition, you may find that when dealing with commercial publications or publications for profit, that you will be able to secure a positive review once you have placed an ad with that particular magazine or newspaper. While all publications do not require you to place an ad before they will write a review, some do, so artist beware. Before your jaws drop consider the following. Most publications for profit make their money from advertising dollars. Since a review of your music brings awareness to you as an artist and your new release, the magazine is helping you gain greater exposure, which may lead to increased CD sales and attendance at your live performances. Hence, some magazines require that you spend advertising dollars before they will write a review of your music worth reading. In turn you receive a review and the magazine will receive advertising dollars; it is a mutually beneficial opportunity.

You should be simultaneously getting music reviews and working on performing live. When you are beginning your career, you will want to focus on perfecting your craft and building a loyal fan base. This is achieved through performing live at every venue possible. If the opportunity presents itself for you to perform in front of 1,000 people do it. Likewise if the opportunity presents itself for you to perform in front of 10 people, do it. The goal is the same, perfecting your craft and building a loyal fan base. With that said here are some ways to make the most out of your live performances. Invite every person on your contact hit list to your live performances. Yes, music writers, DJ's, music retail store managers, club owners, record pool directors, etc. Remember your goal is to get your music heard by potential fans that will buy future releases, your merchandise and support your concerts. One way to get people to try something new is by offering a discount. For example, you may want to sell your full length CD for $7. Some companies have been extremely successful at selling more products by lowering their prices.

By following these simple steps you may turn a live performance into a window of opportunity, begin building a loyal fan base and sell more music and merchandise. Before each performance designate someone (a group member, manager, brother, sister, husband, wife, etc.) to collect names, phone numbers and email addresses of potential fans. Ensure that your representative has the tools necessary for success. For instance, they should have a preprinted mailing list sheet, ink pen, CDs and merchandise to sell as well. Your retail ready CDs should be priced to sell. For instance, your CD should sell a few dollars less than a national recording artist. Therefore, if a Jay-Z or Jill Scott CD sells for $13.99 you may want to sell your music for $9.99. If you did not use any of your money to press your retail ready CDs you can sell your music for much less and still make a profit. Yes, you can **press 1,000 retail ready CDs without using your own money**, but that jewel is reserved for attendees of my dynamic workshop "How to Market & Promote 1,000 Retail Ready CDs Without Using Your Own Money." For dates, times and locations of future seminars visit **www.mt101.com or call 800-963-0949**. Reprint courtesy of JaWar and Music Industry Connection, LLC.

When do I need a manager?

That depends on your personality and business savvy. For instance, some people have a knack for networking, are extremely organized, knowledgeable about the music business and do well in improving and perfecting their craft. So, in the beginning of your career you may not need the service of a manager. However, as you become more commercially successful and are asked to make guest appearances, sought after for endorsements and perform more extensively, you may seek the services of a qualified manager who would help you navigate your growing success.

However, you may need the services of a manager in the early stages of your career to help you identify career goals and objectives, develop your craft, network with music industry professionals and focus on achieving success.

How should I select a qualified manager?

While there are a number of factors that you should consider before choosing a manager a few include the manager's **ability to multi-task, organizational skills, professionalism, knowledge of the business of music, extensive industry contact list and believe in you as an artist.** In addition, the manager should have some knowledge of contract negotiations, how record companies operate and basic bookkeeping and/or accounting skills.

When do I need an attorney?

As an artist you should seek a qualified music attorney before signing any contracts. In many cases if you are a less seasoned or business savvy artist you may also seek a qualified entertainment attorney to help negotiate agreements on your behalf.

How should I select a qualified entertainment attorney?

That depends on what you hire the attorney to do and your career goals and objectives. As an artist you may need contract drafting and negotiation, professional career development and/or contacts to decision makers at record companies, publishing companies and T.V. & film studios, etc. Different entertainment attorneys may provide one or all of these services. Some practical factors to consider before selecting a entertainment attorney include: **how you met the attorney i.e. where they referred to you by a reliable source, the attorneys experience in the music industry, your first instinct (gut feeling) about the attorney (which is probably one of the most important factors of selecting an attorney), how much the attorney charges for his/her services and the connections the attorney has in the music business.**

Of course, there are other factors that should be considered before selecting which attorney you will hire to work for you, but this should get you started when the time is right.

How much do attorney fees cost?

You can expect to pay anywhere from $150/hr to $300/hr for attorney fees. Like many things in life, an attorney's fees are negotiable. It has been my experience that many attorneys are willing to work with aspiring songwriters and artist, if they see that you are serious about your craft and are willing to stay the course. Remember that these attorneys know that you may be the next Jay-Z, Kid Rock, Alicia Keys, Creed, etc. and want the opportunity to represent you. In addition, many of the attorneys had to sacrifice to complete their undergrad and law school studies, so they can appreciate the artist who also has a plan and passion to succeed as they did.

ARTIST'S REVENUE STREAMS

- Publishing Royalties

    1. Mechanical Licenses-CD & Record Sales
    2. Synchronization Licenses-Television, film, commercials i.e. jingles & infomercials
    3. Public Performance-radio airplay
    4. Printed Music-lyric or sheet music

- Touring-concert ticket sales
- Merchandising-t-shirts, hats, shoes, belts, etc. sold at retail stores, concerts, on the Internet, through direct mail and catalog sales
- Guest appearances on other artists songs
- Product and/or service endorsements

PRODUCER'S WORKSHOP

What equipment do I need to begin producing?

Some sound-creating device i.e. a drum machine, drums, keyboard, etc., a amplifier, speakers and recording device. In many instances a computer and the right software may be a substitute for some of the equipment and sounds you will need. Contact some of the music equipment stores in this book to see what they suggest.

How do I insure my equipment?

If you are a homeowner and your equipment is in your house, your equipment should be insured via your homeowners insurance. However, it is always an excellent idea to double-check with your insurance company. If your music equipment is in your apartment, make sure that you have renters insurance to cover the loss in case your equipment is destroyed. Your leasing office may have information on obtaining renter's insurance or you may look for an insurance company in the yellow pages and on-line.

I know of an entertainment attorney that was renting an apartment in Atlanta. Unfortunately, his apartment complex was burned down and all his personal belongings were destroyed. Fortunately, he had renter's insurance and kept photos and receipts for many of his possessions so the insurance company could replace his belongings. No one was hurt in the fire; but only two people including the attorney had renter's insurance. Make sure you insure your music equipment.

In addition, to homeowner's or renter's insurance you may be able to insure your equipment through a music related organization. For instance, through membership in ASCAP, GMIA or NARAS, etc. you may be eligible (qualify) for insurance to cover the loss of your equipment. The companies below specialize in providing insurance for the music industry are listed below:

- Music Pro Insurance Agency
  45 Crossways Park Dr., Woodbury, NY 11797
  P) 800-605-3187 F) 888-290-0302
  www.musicproinsurance.com

- Williams, Turner & Mathis, Inc.
  P.O. Box 450289, Atlanta, GA 31145
  P) 770-934-3248 F) 770-934-3248
  www.wtm-insurance.com
  insurance@wtm-insurance.com

- Robertson Taylor
  315 South Beverly Dr., Suite 201, Beverly Hills, CA 90210
  P) 310-843-0908 F) 310-843-8990
  www.robertson-taylor.com

When do I need an entertainment attorney?

As a music producer you should seek the services of a qualified entertainment attorney before signing any contracts.

What Copyright Forms are needed to protect my music?

You will need Forms PA & Forms SR to protect your music.

Obtain copyright forms through:

- Library of Congress, Copyright Office,
  Register of Copyrights
  101 Independence Avenue, S.E.,
  Washington, D.C. 20559-6000
  Phone: 202-707-3000
  lcweb.loc.gov

- Get a Copyright Kit from Gordon Publishing Company
  Phone: 678-698-7776
  www.copyrightkit.com

How do I protect my company name or logo in Georgia?

Apply for a trademark with the Georgia Secretary of State.

How do I contact the Georgia Secretary of State?

- Office of Secretary of State Corporation Division
  Suite 315, West Tower, 2 MLK Dr., Atlanta, GA 30334
  P) 404-656-2861 F) 404-657-6380
  www.sos.state.ga.us

How do I protect my company name and logo in the U.S.?

To protect an artist stage name, a band's name and/or logo apply for a trademark or servicemark through the U.S. Patent & Trademark Office.

- U.S. Patent and Trademark Office
  General Information Services Division
  Crystal Plaza 3, RM 2 C02
  Washington D.C. 20231
  800-786-9199
  www.uspto.gov

What is a PRO (Performing Rights Organizations)?

A PRO is an organization responsible for collecting & distributing performance royalties (money) to songwriters and music publishers.

- ASCAP-American Society of Composers, Authors and Publishers
  541 Tenth St. NW, #PMB 500, Atlanta, GA 30318
  P) 404-351-1224 F) 404-351-1252
  www.ascap.com

- BMI-Broadcast Music, Inc.
  P.O. Box 19199, Atlanta, GA 31126
  P) 404-261-5151
  www.bmi.com

- SESAC
  55 Music Square East, Nashville, TN 37203
  P) 615-320-0055
  www.sesac.com

RECORDING STUDIOS

As an aspiring music producer you'll want to be able to capture, record and perfect your music production skills easily and inexpensively. That means having access to some basic studio equipment were you can record your raw ideas almost instantaneously. For example, it could be 2:00 am and you might be dreaming of a killer base line with a piano and break-beat on top of it. You might have booked a session for next week at the "BIG" studio, but there is no way your going to remember the base line, piano and break-beat by then. The simple solution, have a drum machine, keyboard/synthesizer, sampler, headphones and/or speakers in your house, so that you can capture, record and perfect your music production skills easily and inexpensively.

In addition, to honing your music production skills easily and inexpensively, owning a pre-production studio will prepare you for recording at a larger facility. **As an aspiring music producer, one of the most important things to remember is that you make hit or hot music, not the equipment. The equipment only allows you to express the arrangement of sounds in your mind and soul.**

There is a wide range of "BIG" studios at your disposal. As a rule of thumb, the least amount of surprises you encounter the better off you are when it comes to recording at these facilities. With that in mind, one of the questions you will want to ask is does the price that you are quoted include the studio engineer's price. Sometimes it does sometimes it doesn't, so remember to ask. In addition, many studios offer block (discount) rates when you book (reserve) say 10 or more hours at a time. So, it is to your advantage to block out time to save money. However, if you are not accustomed to recording for 10 hours then this may be a waste of time and money. Studio prices can range from $25/hr to $150/hr. Remember to bring your own CD-Rs and other record-able devices to the studio. The studio will probably have some on hand, but it will cost you a lot more to buy it from the studio than to bring you own. Hey, the studio is a business, so they are going to make every penny they can. In addition, to the cost you want to ask about the experience of the studio engineer that you will work on your project, what style of music does the studio normally record and if possible to ensure that there is great chemistry between you and the engineer. A few factors to consider before choosing a studio to record in are **studio cost, experience of studio engineer, whether the engineer records your style of music often and chemistry between artist, producer & studio engineer.** Purchasing music equipment and paying for studio time is a business expense. Remember to speak with your tax professional about recouping (getting back) some of these monies when filing your taxes. Below is a list of Recording Studios.

- 1210 Recording Studios
  1210 Spring Street, Atlanta, GA 30309
  P) 404-347-8998

- 500 Grand Studios
  Contact: Carlos Foreman
  1850 Graves Rd., Suite 215, Norcross, GA 30093
  P) 678-969-9121

- Big Cat Studios
  Contact: Tarina
  500 Bishop St., Suite E5, Atlanta, GA 30318
  P) 404-603-8229 P) 404-641-7210

- Blackberry Recording Studios
  3141 Eat Ponce De Leon, Scottsdale, GA 30079
  P) 404-687-0920

- Capstone Musicworks
  Contact: Stacey Wallace
  8385 Cherokee Blvd. Suite 200, Douglasville, GA 30135
  P) 770-947-3534 Cell) 678-698-7956
  www.capstonemusicworks.com
  swallace@capstonemusicworks.com

- Down 4 Life Recording Studios
  5127 Old National Hwy, Atlanta, GA 30349
  P) 404-766-7377

- Electronika Recording Studios
  2963 Stone Road, Atlanta, GA 30344
  P) 404-766-0288

- Evolution Recording Studios
  Contact: Reggie Regg
  3131 Campbelton Rd., Suite-H, Atlanta, GA 30311
  P) 404-840-3846

- **Golden Boy Recording Studios**
  Contact: Ray Hamilton
  5319 Old National Hwy, College Park, GA 30349
  P) 404-684-5999 F) 404-684-5973

- House 21 Entertainment Recording Studio
  Contact: Mike
  2100 Drake Court, Lithonia, GA 30058
  P) 678-508-3742

- Joi Recording Studios
  2356 Park Central Blvd., Decatur, GA 30035
  P) 678-418-9973

- Lakefront Studios
  Contact: Benjamin Cornthwaite
  P) 770-602-0995 F) 770-602-1206 M) 404-925-5583
  www.lakefrontstudios.com

- Maze Recording Studio
  Contact: Derrick
  2963 Lambert Dr., Atlanta, GA 30324
  Cell) 770-633-5747 P) 678-428-3437

- Paradise Recording Studio
  Contact: James Gray
  1651 Link Overlook, Atlanta, GA 30088
  P) 404-351-0086

- Red Swan Studio
  Contact: Juare'z Lee
  5658 Riverdale Rd., Unit-Q, College Park, GA 30349
  P) 770-909-9779

- Patchwerk Recording Studios
  1094 Hemphill, Atlanta, GA 30318
  P) 404-874-9880

- Reel to Reel Recording Studios
  1440 Dutch Valley Place, Suite 790, Atlanta, GA 30324
  P) 404-817-3883

RECORDING MUSIC RETAIL STORES

- Atlanta Band Centre
  Contact: Stacy Nall
  S. Dekalb Plaza
  2746 Candler Rd., Decatur, GA 30034
  P) 404-212-0420 F) 404-244-0811
  www.atlantabandcentre.com
  bandcenter2746@yahoo.com

- Atlanta Band Centre
  Contact: Stacy Nall
  Evanswood Center
  2928-B Evansmill Rd., Lithonia, GA 30058
  P) 678-526-0909
  www.atlantabandcentre.com
  bandcenter2928@yahoo.com

- Atlanta Band Centre
  Contact: Stacy Nall
  5055-B Memorial Dr., Stone Mountain, GA 30083
  P) 404-477-DRUM (3786)
  www.atlantabandcentre.com
  bandcenter5055@yahoo.com

- Atlanta Discount Music, Inc.
  Contact: Bill Erwin
  4934 Peachtree Rd., Chamblee, GA 30341
  P) 770-457-3400 P) 866-322-6220
  www.atlantadiscountmusic.com

- Atlantamusicbrokers.com

- Avata Events Group
  471 Glen Iris Dr., Atlanta, GA 30308

P) 404-589-9450 F) 404-589-9451
www.avataeventsgroup.com

- Guitar Center (2)
  1485 Northeast Expressway, Atlanta, GA 30329
  www.guitarcenter.com

- Magic Audio-ATL
  Contact: Ben Cornthwaite
  204 14th St. NW, Atlanta, GA 30318
  P) 404-249-6336 F) 404-249-9422
  www.magicaudio.com

- Musiq World
  Contact: Robin
  1901 Montreal Road, Ste 137, Tucker, GA 30084
  P) 678-249-5527

- National Sound & Video
  6500 McDonough Dr., Norcross, GA 30093
  P) 770-447-0101 F) 770-447-1355
  www.natlsound.com
  curtis@natlsound.com

- Pro Music Outlet
  Contact: Tony or Jackie
  4727 Memorial Dr., Decatur, GA 30032
  P) 404-294-5100
  www.promusicoutlet.com

- Sound Associates
  Contact: Amy
  560-F Amsterdam Ave., Atlanta, GA 30306
  P) 404-724-9050 F) 404-724-9891
  www.soundassociates.net
  info@soundassociates.net

CD/DVD/VINYL DUPLICATORS

- A Black Clan Distribution & Manufacturing Inc.
  Contact: Juan C. Williams
  P) 877-706-7316 P) 770-907-8665 F) 770-907-9216
  www.ablackclan.com
  juan@ablackclan.com

- Atlanta Manufacturing Group
  83 Walton St., Third Floor, Atlanta, GA 30303
  P) 404-230-9559 F) 230-9558
  www.amgcds.com
  info@amgcds.com

- Creative Media
  2783 Senecca Trail, Duluth, GA 30096-6298
  P) 770-447-8137
  www.creativemedia.com
  sales@creativemedia.com

- MDS
  824-B Memorial Dr., Atlanta, GA 30316
  P) 404-584-0372 F) 404-584-9406
  www.mdsincsonline.com

- Mindzai
  1139 Euclid Avenue, Atlanta, GA 30307
  P) 404-577-8484 F) 404-577-5895
  www.mindzai.net

- ON4 Productions
  684 Antone St., NW Suite 110, Atlanta, GA 30318
  P) 888-710-5157 P) 404-603-9900 F) 404-351-7775
  www.on4prod.com

- Project 70 Audio Services
  433 Bishop St., NW Suite CD, Atlanta, GA 30310
  P) 404-875-7000 F) 404-875-7007
  www.project70.com

- Straight from the Soul
  Contact: Corey Bivens
  5741 Wells Circle, Stone Mountain, GA 30087
  P) 770-413-2464
  soulent@aol.com

- Yourmusiconcd.com
  Contact: Suwat
  421 A-1 Pike Blvd., Lawrenceville, GA 30045
  P) 877-442-0933 P) 678-442-0933 F) 678-377-9765
  sns@yourmusiconcd.com

PRINTERS FOR FLYERS & CD-INSERTS

- Ananse Creative
  Contact: Salah Ananse
  P) 404-344-9343 P) 678-592-4795
  www.ananse creative.com
  ansecreative@bellsouth.net

- Digiprint
  2395 Pleasantdale Rd., Suite 4-B, Atlanta, GA 30340
  P) 770-368-2060 F) 770-368-9943

- Extreme Media
  1440 Dutch Valley Pl., Suite 160
  P) 404-815-0553 F) 404-815-0314
  www.extremeatlanta.com

- Identity Graphics & Printing
  Contact: Ira Watkins
  254 E. Paces Ferry Rd., Atlanta, GA 30305
  P) 404-417-9777
  www.identitypress.net

- Small Business Promotions, Inc.
  P.O. Box 1348, Lithonia, GA 30058
  P) 678-886-8792 P) 770-557-0938

www.designsnprint.com
orders@designsnprint.com

- Star Shooters
  277-B East Paces Ferry Rd, Atlanta, GA 30305
  P) 404-869-8844 F) 404-869-8833

- Southern Poster Printing
  3862 Stevens Ct., Tucker, GA
  P) 888-872-8194 P) 404-872-8194

- Southern Stamp & Stencil
  428 Edgewood Ave., Atlanta, GA 30312
  P) 800-241-0985 P) 404-522-4431
  www.southernstamp.com
  info@southernstamp.com

MUSIC CONFERENCES

Music Conferences are a fantastic way to network, negotiate and know the business of music. By attending a music conference you have the ability to create windows of opportunity for yourself. This is achieved by first having a clearly identifiable goal. For instance, your goal may be to network with aspiring singers, songwriters and artist or to gather contact information from other industry decision-makers.

In addition, some music conferences have a T.V. and film component, which is a fantastic way to network with decision-makers who may be willing and able to get your music placed on T.V. and/or in a movie. As a music producer your goal should be to get your music heard in as many outlets as possible. Not only does this make you a more marketable music producer, but it also creates additional streams of revenue for you. Below is a list of music conferences to consider attending.

- A&R Music1.com, LLC.
  2132 Sara Ashley Way - Suite 300 Lithonia, GA 30058
  P) 770-686-9100
  www.armusic1.com

- Atlantis Music Conference
  1339 Canton Rd., Suite E, Marietta, GA 30066
  P) 770-499-8600 F) 770-499-8650
  www.atlantismusic.com

- **MUSIC THERAPY 101**
  P.O. Box 52682, Atlanta, GA 30355
  800-963-0949
  www.mt101.com
  questions@mt101.com

MASTERING FACILITIES

- Bull Moon Mastering
  P) 770-522-8770 F) 770-522-0621

- Glenn Schick Mastering
  3264 Shallowford Rd., Atlanta, GA 30341
  P) 770-451-1314 F) 770-457-5243

- Griffin Mastering
  1051 Woodland Ave, Atlanta, GA 30316
  P) 404-622-5102
  www.mindspring.com/~gminc/
  gminc@mindspring.com

- HDQTRZ Digital Studios
  Contact: Earle Holder
  P) 404-643-8213
  www.hdqtrz.com
  earle@hdqtrz.com

- Inspiremedia
  Contact: John Penn
  P) 678-887-5678
  inspiremedia@comcast.net

- Taj Mahal
  P) 404-282-9777

WEBSITES OF INTEREST

- www.breakbeatvault.com
- www.futureproducers.com
- www.justbeats.biz
- www.dynamicproducer.com

MUSIC PRODUCERS

- AC Akalawu (Raham)
  SoulVersive Productions
  2896 Highland Park Drive, Stone Mountain, GA 30087
  P) 404-388-0040 F) 770-498-0954
  www.soulversive.com
  cheryl@soulversive.com
  Style: Neo-Soul/R&B/Rap

- BeatSmith Media
  Contact: Milton Walker
  P.O. Box 1582, Marietta, GA 30061
  P) 770-912-3767
  www.beatsmith.com
  mwalker@beatsmith.com
  Style: Hip Hop/Rap

- Brandon Batts
  Soul House Entertainment
  883 Fayettevile Rd., Atlanta, GA 30316
  P) 770-256-7901
  Style: R&B/Neo-Soul/Hip Hop

- Business
  The Future Productions
  605 Amal Dr. SW Buliding 57, Atlanta, GA 30315
  P) 404-964-7178
  mrbd082004@yahoo.com
  Style: Rap/R&B/Futuristic Sound

- F. Angel (Levance Mcqueen)
  Sydwynda(Sidewinder)Productionz
  503 Summerview Dr., Stone Mountain, Ga 30083
  P) 404-723-0574
  www.audiovizion.com
  f.angel@audiovizion.com
  Style: R&B/Hip-Hop/Alternative

- Hartbeatz
  Southern Trees Film Group Inc.
  3535 Suite 520-155 Peachtree Rd N.E.,
  Atlanta, GA 30308
  P) 678-887-4129
  gabrielhart@hotmail.com
  Style: Film Scores/Rap/Voice-Overs

- Hotep
  Skinnymen Productions
  404-294-7165
  www.skinnymen.com
  info@skinnymen.com
  Style: Old School Hip-Hop/R&B/Spoken Word

- Isaac "Zeek" Underwood
  Urban Plug Management
  3070 Windward Plaza Suite F-140, Alpharetta, GA 30005
  Inside ATL: 770.851.0698
  Inside ATL: 800.240.2392
  www.urbanplug.com
  zeek@urbanplug.com
  Styles: Hip-Hop/R&B/ANY

- Jae Ellis
  P) 770-572-2404
  www.jaeellis.com
  Style: Hip Hop/Rap/R&B

- Joan Cartwright
  FYI COMMUNICATIONS, INC.
  2644 Graywall Street, East Point, GA 30344
  P) 404-767-9699 C) 954-655-6345
  www.fyicomminc.com
  Style: Jazz/Blues/Hip Hop

- Jonathan Burtner
  Burtner Audio Labs
  3914 Madison Bend, Suite 101, Kennesaw, GA 30144
  P) 770-590-1989 F) 810-815-0920
  www.jburtner.com
  jburtner@jburtner.com
  Style: Rock/Eclectic/Experimental

- Jorma Starratt
  Attica Sound, LLC
  441 hale lane, Athens, GA 30607
  P) 706.227.8991 C) 404.431.4969 F) 360.248.6158
  www.atticasound.com
  jorma@atticasound.com
  Style: Hip Hop

- Kelly Keeling
  Serge Entertainment
  6918 Heritage Place, Acworth, GA 30102
  P) 678-445-0006 F) 678/494-9269
  www.serge.org/kelly_keeling
  SergeEnt@aol.com
  Style: Metal/Rap/Alternative

- K-RAW

Groundbreakin Entertainment
8491 Hospital Dr. #177 Douglasville, Ga.30134-2412
P) 678-777-8023
k-raw@mail.com
Style: Hip Hop/R&B/Soul

- Linked Productions
  Contact: Big Yo, Al-C, Kebu
  P) 877-706-7316 P) 770-907-8665 P) 503-232-6724
  evredark@ablackclan.com
  Style: HipHop/ R&B/Gospel

- Montayne Farrar
  Iconoclast, Inc
  1147 Forest Vale Lane U8, Norcross, GA 30093
  P) 404-695-0150 P) 404-327-6136
  http://iconoclast.freehomepage.com/
  montaynef@trx.com

- Richard "Payday" Renix
  Mack Rodd Productions
  1812 Summit Lake Dr., Stone Mountain, GA 30083
  P) 770-413-3852 Cell) 770-912-4591
  Payday13@bellsouth.net
  Style: Hip Hop/R&B/Rock

- Rock Most
  Red Reign Studios
  2579 Park Central Blvd., Decatur, GA 30035
  P) 678-418-5144 F) 678-418-5145
  www.redreignstudios.com
  jhibad@redreignstudios.com
  Style: Hip Hop/R&B/Soul

- Romeo LaShawn
  New Era Productions, Inc.
  3150 DeerField Way, Rex, GA 30274
  P) 678-886-6279 F) 770-736-3809
  newera14@aol.com

Style: Hip Hop/R&B/Soul

- Science Fiction
  Shaman Work Recordings
  P) 678 945 9139
  www.angryrobotrecords.com
  sci@angryrobotrecords.com

- Sharaab
  UNDO
  659 Auburn Ave. Suite #130, Atlanta, GA 30312
  P) 404-931-3263
  sharaab@hotmail.com
  www.undocorp.com
  Style: Electronica/Drum&Bass/Ambient

- Torrey "T-Beats" Brown
  2 Dove Production Enterprises, Inc.
  2817 Crest Ridge Way, Marietta, GA 30060
  P) 678-556-9562
  globee2dove@bellsouth.net
  Style: Rap/Gospel/R&B

- Tariq Robinson
  Peahole Sounds
  1940 South Hidden Hills Parkway
  Stone Mountain, GA 30088
  P) 770-686-PEAS
  www.peaholesounds.com
  beats@peaholesounds.com
  Style: Metal/Hip-Hop/R&B

How should a producer market their tracks?

1. Create & distribute a promotional instrumental CD; make sure your contact information is printed on all the CDs you hand out.

2. Create a website with streaming & downloadable tracks.

3. Place your website address on every promotional item you hand out, including business cards.

4. Create mix CDs with the hottest artists rapping or singing over your tracks.

5. Submit your tracks to artists, managers, music publishers and attorneys that are seeking new music.

PRODUCER'S REVENUE STREAM

As a music producer you're in a unique position to earn an unlimited amount of money over time. The easiest way is to sell your tracks to the highest bidder. While selling your tracks to the highest bidder may turn you a quick profit, it may not be the most profitable way to earn your money. What is more profitable is to create opportunities where you generate multiple streams of revenue from the same track over time. This simply means you would earn money whenever your song is played.

Some of the ways your song may generate additional money is through music publishing, i.e. public performance, mechanical licenses, synchronization licenses and printed music, video games, downloadable ring tones, wireless devices, webscating and digital performance royalties.

Mechanical royalties are paid from the sale of CDs and/or records. For example, as a producer you may get 3 points or 3% of the CD suggested retail price minus 10% or 15%. The ten or fifteen percent would go toward manufacturing & packaging the CD. Performance royalties are paid whenever a song you produced is played for the public. For instance, if the song is played on radio, t.v., cable, concert halls, and other music outlets you would be entitled to performance publishing royalties (money). These royalties are normally collected in the United States by three performance rights organizations or PROs. The PROs are ASCAP (American Society of Composers, Authors & Publishers), BMI (Broadcast Music Inc.) and SESAC (formerly known as the Society of European Stage Authors & Composers). Video games are also an excellent way to generate additional revenue. Many of the top game makers now have A&R (Artist & Repertoire) Departments.

Synchronization licenses are issued when your music is used in television, film or commercials i.e. jingles and infomercials. Depending on the popularity of the song, how your song is used and your clout as a music producer/composer, you may structure a deal where you receive a flat fee for how your song is to be played, a royalty each time the television program, film or commercial is aired or a combination of both. Structuring a deal that would pay a royalty each time your song is played would put you on the fast track to generating multiple steams of royalty revenue.

Printed music royalties are generated whenever your song is sold as sheet music. When the sheet music or lyrics of your song are displayed on a website, you are entitled to a royalty, especially if the website is generating income; an issue your entertainment attorney should address in depth with you.

Downloadable ring tones for cell phones and other wireless devices, is potentially a huge source of additional income. Whenever someone downloaded one of your tracks you should receive a royalty. Imagine receiving 10 cent per download; with millions of cell phone and wireless device users worldwide your earning potential is magnified. If you're interested in making your songs available as downloadable ring tones you may call me and I will put you in direct contact with one of my industry sources. There is a small fee for this contact, but with magnified earnings potential it will be worth every nickel. For details contact me toll-free at 800-963-0949 or jawar@mt101.com

Webcasting & digital performance royalties are relatively new, but the money making potential for music producers is enormous. To ensure you receive your webcasting & digital performance royalties you will need to send Soundexchange a Producers Letter of Direction. As a the copyright owner of your music you may be entitled to additional webcasting royalties under the Copyright Act. Remember that selling your tracks for a flat fee is only one way to generate money from your music. As a music producer you could create multiple income streams through music publishing, video games, downloadable ring tones, wireless devices, webcasting and digital performance royalties.

PRODUCER'S REVENUE STREAM

- Publishing royalties

    1. Mechanical Licenses-CD & Record Sales
    2. Synchronization Licenses-Television, film, commercials i.e. jingles & infomercials
    3. Public Performance-radio airplay
    4. Printed Music-lyric or sheet music

- Touring-concert ticket sales
- Merchandising-t-shirts, hats, shoes, belts, etc. sold at retail stores, concerts, on the Internet, through direct mail and catalog sales
- Guest appearances on other artists songs
- Product and/or service endorsements
- Video Games

- Downloadable Ring tones & other wireless devices
- Webcasting & Digital Performance Royalties

MANAGER'S CORNER

What skills do I need to succeed as a manager?

As an artist manager a few of the many skills you should possess include the ability to seek and develop star talent, be extremely organized, professional, know the business of music, have extensive contacts in the industry and genre of which you seek to develop star talent and above all, be honest and truly believe in the artist you are managing.

As a manager you may have to be a husband, wife, mother, father, brother, sister and friend to the artist you are managing. Meaning at various times in the artists career you may have to play the role of any one of these persons to comfort and support your artist.

In addition, the manager should have some knowledge of contract negotiations, how record companies operate, basic bookkeeping and/or accounting skills and be computer and Internet literate.

What are the three types of managers?

1. **Artist Manager**-An artist manager may be responsible for finding and developing star talent and navigating an artist's career to create and maximize "fame equity."

2. **Business Manager**-A business manager normally handles the financial affairs of the artist to ensure that the artist spends less money than they make.

In addition, the business manager may help to diversify the artist's financial assets i.e. investing in real estate, the stock market, bonds and other businesses, to ensure that the artist is able to maintain a certain standard of living and invest money for retirement.

NOTE: The artist should always write their own checks or have a system that allows the artists to closely monitor the business manager's activity. Trust is fantastic; accountability is better.

3. **Road Manager**-A road manager is responsible for a number of tasks while the artist is touring. For example, the road manager will ensure that all the contractual arrangements made with the venue have been met. In addition, the road manager will ensure that the artist arrives promptly for all the promotional appearances, such as in-stores, radio, print media and other engagements to promote the tour.

When do I need an entertainment attorney?

A manager should seek a qualified entertainment attorney before signing any contracts. In some instances a manager may also seek the services of an attorney to negotiate contracts on their behalf.

How much money are artist managers typically paid?

Artist managers typically get between 5% to 25% of an artist's gross earnings.

Who pays the manager?

The artist normally pays the manager. Remember the artist manager works for the artist.

May the manager also be the artist's attorney?

Yes, although in some instances it may be a conflict of interest. For example, since there should be a written contract between the artist and manager, the attorney who is also the artist manager may not draft (write) and execute (make happen) the best contract for the artist between the artist and manager, since the attorney is also the manager.

MANAGEMENT ORGANIZATIONS

- Indie Managers Association
  www.indiemanagers.com
  indie@indiemanagers.com

- International Music Managers Forum
  www.immf.net

- Music Managers Forum
  www.mmfus.com

- National Conference of Personal Managers
  www.ncopm.com
  askncopm@ncopm.com

MANAGEMENT COMPANIES

- Alliance Artist
  1225 N. Meadow Pkwy, Suite 100, Roswell, GA 30076
  P) 770-663-4240 F) 770-663-8757

- Artist Control Management
  685 Lambert Dr., NE, Atlanta, GA 30324-4125
  P) 404-733-5511 F) 404-733-5512

- Artist Management International
  P.O. Box 671837, Atlanta, GA 30006
  P) 770-428-5484 F) 770-514-9710

- Brash Management
  Contact: Richard Dunn
  658 11th St., Atlanta, GA 30318
  P) 678-904-4790
  www.brashmusic.com
  dunn@brashmusic.com

- Brown Cat, Inc.
  400 Foundry St., Athens, GA 30601
  P) 706-354-8301 F) 770-369-1631

- Dailey's Entertainment
  Contact: Moses Daily
  P.O. Box 13365, Atlanta, GA 30324
  P) 404-239-8062 F) 404-241-8869
  mosesdaily@aol.com

- Daycare Management & Consulting
  Contact: Brad McDonald
  450 Ashburton Ave., Atlanta, GA 30317
  P) 404-687-8711 F) 404-378-8542 Cell) 404-277-9838
  daycaremgmt@mindspring.com

- Elevation Management
  Contact: E. Anthony Daniel
  5300 Memorial Dr., Suite 201 E, Stone Mountain, GA 30083
  P) 404-508-9017
  eadaniel@bellsouth.net

- Family Tree Management
  2356 Park Central Blvd., Decatur, GA 30317
  P) 678-418-9973

- Flip Management
  396 Autumn Dr., Riverdale, GA 30274
  P) 770-210-5299 F) 404-246-4012

- Goldston & Associates Entertainment Management
  Contact: Nathaniel Russell Goldston IV "Russ"
  82 Piedmont Ave., Atlanta, GA 30303
  P) 404-550-6164
  nbreden@yahoo.com

- Impact Artist Management
  P.O. Box 347265, Atlanta, GA 30334
  P) 404-435-5613

- J-Pat Management
  Contact: Jonetta Patton
  3996 Pleasantdale Rd., #104-A, Doraville, GA 30340
  P) 770-416-8619 F) 770-409-2385

- Jess Rosen
  3423 Piedmont Rd., #200, Atlanta, GA 30305
  P) 404-237-7700 F) 404-237-5260

- Mad Money Entertainment
  2892 Mountain Industrial Blvd., Alpharetta, GA 30084
  P) 770-938-2277 F) 770-938-2199

- Marvelous Enterprises
  1676 Defoors Circle, Atlanta, GA 30318
  P) 404-367-9122 F) 404-367-9123

- Midnight Management
  Contact: David Freeman
  4247 Orchard Grove, Stone Mountain, GA 30083
  P) 404-508-9690
  Fortknox76@yahoo.com

- Music Business Associates
  Contact: Dominic
  933 Wild Wood, Stone Mountain, GA 30083
  P) 770-374-5114
  musicbusinessassociates@aol.com

- Nico Don Projects
  Vonico "Nico Don" Johnson
  2768 Browntown Rd., NW, Atlanta, GA 30318
  P) 404-668-5444
  nicodon2002@yahoo.com

- **Own Music**
  Contact: Dayo Adebiyi
  2451 Cumberland Pkwy, Suite 3516,
  Atlanta, GA 30339
  P) 770-413-7440
  www.ownmusic.com
  dayo.adebiyi@ownmusic.com

- Priceless Music Management
  Artist Roster: Kelly Price
  2771 Lawrenceville Hwy #206, Atlanta, GA
  P) 770-724-1933 F) 770-724-1987

- The Woodland Entertainment Group, Inc.
  Contact: Kirk D. Woods
  2870 Peachtree Rd., Suite 226, Atlanta, GA 30305
  P) 404-378-0334 F) 404-378-8120
  woodlandent@hotmail.com

- Triple Platinum Management
  1 Biscayne Dr., Penthouse #709, Atlanta, GA 30309
  P) 404-350-3212 F) 404-350-8393

MANAGEMENT BOOKS

- All Area Access:
  Personal Management for Unsigned Musicians
  By Marc Davison

- Business of Artist Management
  By Xavier M. Frascogna Jr. & H. Lee Hetherington

- Choosing a Manager
  By John E. Kali

- Managing Your Band
  By Dr. Stephen Marcone

- The Game of Hip Hop Artist Management
  By Walt Goodridge
  www.hiphopbiz.com

Interview with Dayo & Al of Own Music

JaWar: What's your name?

Dayo: Dayo Adebiyi

Al: I'm Al Thrash

JaWar: How long have each of you been in the music industry?

Dayo: Since '95

JaWar: How about you Al?

Al: About 10 years

JaWar: How did you get started in the music business?

Dayo: I go back to junior high, high school, rapping with classmates and hanging out. I'm from the west coast, so I came up right around the time where for whatever reason the west coast was hot and there were a lot of acts out there, so you were more than likely to have friends who ran in different circles with artist who were getting deals and what not. Hieroglyphics was one of those camps that I ran with back then. I focused on my school and my interest in music because of my social circle. I wanted to see what kind of went on behind the scenes and was really interested [in the business of music]. So that's kind of what got me into it. In terms of working, once I got out here and went to Morehouse in 92', I had some other friends from California who were here working in the industry doing street teamwork, consulting and promotions. Hanging around them and just learning the lifestyle that you could achieve and reach. Not so much about the money but setting your own schedule and the freedom.

JaWar: How about you Al?

Al: With me it started coming out of high school, freshman year of college, I had some friends that ran parties. Back in '92, '93 it was nothing like you see in Atlanta now, with the whole party thing. There were one or two guys, who'd do a party Christmas Night, Thanksgiving Night and maybe two parties over the summer. These guys were friends of my sister. They knew I was a freshman in the AUC (Atlanta University Center) and I could attract a lot of people for them in terms of freshmen and sophomores, so I just started doing parties and that more or less got me acclimated to promotions. When people see you around passing some flyers then a lot of people come to you and they come to your party. I knew that record labels gave out music and they love to know that we could get a crowd together for their artist. So I started calling [record companies] and getting CDs and posters to give out. So that's how it started. Arista was the first company I called and they were really taking care of us back then.

JaWar: Both of you mentioned that you've been to college. Is that where you met?

Al: Mmmmmm yeah, yeah!

Dayo: We both went to Morehouse and I'd see Al around campus. I was an intern at BMG and he started working with Arista and that's when we linked up.

Al: It was one of those things where I knew Dayo did something with music on campus. I would come into a marketing class while he was leaving. You always had that 10 or 15 minutes of talk time, 'have you heard this new CD da da da...' and we just kept that going and that's what brought us together.

JaWar: Do you think that college has prepared you for the music industry in terms of artist management?

Al: I definitely think it has. I think that college has prepared me for a lot, everything that I do in life "really" but specifically music. One thing about college is it took a whole city and shrunk it into a campus. So to me, the AU (Atlanta University) Center where there were three or four schools there to me that was a replica of Atlanta, even more so a replica of the US, because you got people coming from all over. And so on that campus you have artists, producers, business people, rich kids, poor kids, etc. So just in learning how to deal with people with different lifestyles and backgrounds, embrace creativity, see all the different kinds of things from opposite sides of the country or whatever; I do feel that it prepared me for working in the industry.

Dayo: I have a little different take on that. I think school prepared me for what's necessary in terms of trying to be upwardly mobile within the entertainment industry, in terms of networking skills and things like that. I think in a campus environment there are not nearly as many individuals who are going to be out to do whatever they have to do to get to their objective. Whereas in the [music] industry you'll find it's so cut throat and scrupulous it doesn't matter they'll [people in the music industry] run right through you if they have the opportunity. They don't try to create their own business, so in that regard, college and framework didn't necessarily prepare me for that experience but our work experience as well. School enabled us to at least get a taste of what was to come and some of the transition.

JaWar: If you could sum it up in a sentence or two, how would you define artist management?

Al: I would define it as the necessary business that's needed to bring creativity to the marketplace. Meaning managing an artist or producer, everything from label or business relations for this artist or producer, dealing with whatever entity is releasing the music managing or taking care of the process of doing work and of work ethics. Everything from how well their music is recorded to the types of outlets that you try to get it out in just managing that entire process and making sure that the artist is aware of all of the steps in the value chain so that as your creating the music that goes ten different places, they are aware that this person, this entity has to do this to it so we have to make sure, before it gets out the door, we know business wise, publishers, where it's going, sales wise, dealing with the label, where its going and what needs to be done with that music to get it there.

JaWar: What skills does a person need to become an artist manager or to succeed as an artist manager?

Dayo: I think you need a lot of interpersonal skills. It's a relationship business. You go furthest based upon the way you hold your head above rising waters. I also feel that managing an artist is basically a lot of faith, hoping that you're going to be guiding them right, steering them and also have a vision of your own that should coincide with your client to get that person or group where they want to be. [As a manager] you're a service provider. You want to provide the best service. It helps get you to your objectives without loosing who you are as well.

Al: A lot of it is empowering the artist or our client with many of the things that we're doing. Many times you look at an artist manager relationship and the artist is just doing music, they are clueless to what happens once they hand that CD or mix tape over. I find that when an artist is empowered about the industry and about the marketplace then that makes for a better working relationship and things tend to thrive little bit better.

JaWar: Could you give three or four responsibilities of an artist manager?

Dayo: Representation, business management, empowerment and education.

JaWar: How bout you Al, would you say that about the same?

Al: Yeah, I would definitely say the same and another major responsibility about artist management is getting the money.

JaWar: Explain that a little bit.

Al: When the artist makes the decision that they are going to make music professionally and this is how they're going to eat and live, it's different types of avenues out there to exploit a copyright just to make the most money and get a possible offer off of the copyright, meaning a song or whatever. It doesn't just come to you, you put an album out, that's great, its up to us to seek out soundtrack opportunities, commercials, just get to places where we can make the most money possible for our artist and in turn for ourselves. It doesn't happen from us just going about our day to day [business], we have to be very proactive about it.

JaWar: Could you give one example of how you were able to do that for one of your previous or current clients i.e. one specific example of how you were able to

take a song they did and actually use it beyond the CD that they released?

Al: Yeah! For example, Killer Mike's, "Action Song" was the lead single for his album. The song itself was not hugely accepted radio wise, but the format of the song, the tempo and feel made it very appealing to the video game culture. It has that kind of feel and it's on Madden 4 the EA Sports Game as the lead song. In some ways you have to play the cards you're dealing with; hopefully if you can keep your hand alive then something is going to happen.

JaWar: I'm going to go back to that because our readers want to know the specifics without getting into the menial aspects. How were you able to get Killer Mike's song onto that video game? I mean did you call the person [at EA Sports], did they seek you out, and how did it work? What were the specific steps you took on getting the song used?

Dayo: Al and I really started trying to heighten the awareness and profile of the artist himself and subsequently his music. It started prior to the release of his album. EA sports and most of the video game companies now have separate music departments and even A&R's that are assigned specifically to oversee the talent and music that they put on these games. And this particular A&R was amongst a circle so we linked up and reached out and saw that sometime earlier he was already aware of Killer Mike and once the album came out he was able to hear all the music he felt that that song fit his game Madden 4. Mike had done the previous Madden, Madden 3 and had success with that. [The Madden Game] ships about 4 million copies out the gate [so your not] going to deny it but he reached out to us, because he'd been aware of Killer Mike.

Al: In reaching out to us he identified a song amongst a few songs that we presented and that song seemed to work, but we just needed to make some changes, obviously to really fit that format. Mike already had a lot of football references in the song but in speaking with the A&R he let us know what kind of things Mike really needed to draw upon. We got back with Mike and said well this is a great opportunity they want accept it the way it is now, but we could go back and do X, Y & Z, it could be a big hit on the video game scene. We went back to the lab he made a few changes on it lyric wise and we sent it out and it was exactly what they were looking for.

JaWar: Was there a lot of red tape in terms of possible clearances with Aquemini Records, given that is the label that he was or is signed to right now?

Dayo: At that point, there wasn't so much from what I can remember and I think a lot of that really is due to when this kind of went down; right after the album came out, probably a month or so after the album came out. Unfortunately sales wise that album didn't meet any of our expectations. You know it sold, but for the sweat we put into it, two years working on it, of course we wanted it to sell in a day what it sold in those two or three months. Just for that reason here's an opportunity to keep that artist out there [in the public light] and legally it is PA and so, you know, we're going to get paid for it. So, it wasn't so much red tape as I hear some other situations may come up and the label is like 'no', you know...

JaWar: How did you meet Killer Mike?

Al: I actually went to High School with Killer Mike.

JaWar: What High School was that?

Al: Frederick Douglass High School here in Atlanta. Yeah, so we actually graduated together. I had known him since around 8th or 9th grade. We stayed in contact. Mike went to Morehouse as well, so we stayed in contact there, I knew he was doing music and I started doing music as well. Over the years I ended up moving to Nashville doing some work out there. We lost contact for a year or two then we caught back up. I knew he was doing music. Really his sheer talent allowed him to pop up on the Outkast album. He just rapped for Big Boi one day and they were like 'I got to have you'. I definitely give him props for that because his sheer talent got him to where he is now. We just stayed in contact he kept it going and he got into the deal situation where we had an opportunity for us to work with him and really get him developed.

JaWar: How do you feel that you were able to help develop Killer Mike's career? Taking him from just rapping on the corner, if you will, to rapping for Outkast, to maybe helping him get signed, closing the deal and doing EA sports?

Dayo: I think our biggest benefit was probably giving him some understanding as to what the industry is all about. Not necessarily the parties and long nights at the studio, but the true work that goes into it from the grass roots approach. He had been surrounded by half these guys who were all multi-platinum plus artists! It had been a long time since they had a real developing artist go through the steps of development, so I think exposing him and letting him understand what is necessary to break as a new artist in the market is invaluable as well as giving him a perspective in his own right. How he viewed things and what he personally chose to make his path so he's not a carbon copy of someone else. He tried to create his own identity, which we value more than anything else.

Al: We had a lot of relationships from our past dealings in the industry at BMG, with DJ's, retailers and record storeowners across the country. So once the album came through the pipeline we had people along those lines in various markets. I lived in Nashville for three years and Nashville was the number two-radio market for a single, the relationships that we had with radio in Nashville got a lot of sales for Mike's release.

JaWar: How does a manager get paid, how do you get paid?

Dayo: What we've done is we've set up a company, that's how we look at our artists or our producers, we set these companies up and we get percentages of that. Generally that's 15%-20%. We really try to look at the people who deal with us as almost media companies in their own right. Everyone's trying to get their word, their voice out and it speaks kind of wide. They're media companies just like TNT or CBS.

JaWar: That 15%-20% is that Gross or Net of what those companies bring in?

Dayo: That's gross.

Al: And ideally in terms of at what point the artist is in his career, if we are actually developing this artist for the sake of getting a record deal and go and land a deal then that percentage of the deal as well. It tends to still be about 15%- 20% when we go and land a deal. That's obviously if, you're talking about a huge budget, that's a big payoff. Along the way, that is if you did shows, if they license a song, if they asked for an appearance etc. that's 15% - 20% of that. It's in our interest to be pro-active, make as many calls as we can make, get as much work done because artists really when we would ideally want our artist working 350 days out the year.

JaWar: What's the name of your company?

Dayo: Own Music

JaWar: If people wanted to get in contact with you, how would they do that?

Dayo: They can email al.thrash@ownmusic.com as well as dayo.adebiyi@ownmusic.com or they can call us on 770-413-7440.

JaWar: Any closing comments?

Al: One thing I would say is right now Own Music is managing a 14year old name Shorthand his 21-year-old brother is his producer, One Will productions. We've been working with them for about 2 years now, they just moved to Atlanta, so we're very excited about that. We're looking to fill that void of that younger artist right now, whether he's not really out there, but we're doing some big boy stuff, that's what the music is going to be focused on in 2004. We are looking at continuing to expand our line up.

Dayo: I'd just like to note one reason why I started the company, it's like, we were going to venture away from BMG, which was a comfortable check at the time because we really believed in the artists. We try to make certain that we keep the integrity with all of our clients and the integrity of the music and it's something that they create and they own that's why we created the name Own Music. When people in the shower singing or in the basement cooking up beats, walking the walk humming, we want them out and we will market them, promote that in a way that would benefit them. Not just anything, like the large distributors, Sony, BMG, WEA, or whatever. In a lot of ways music is like that, for a young kid specifically to get out given current situations and we want to make certain that they have the opportunity to do that.

JaWar: Appreciate it

MANAGER'S REVENUE STREAM

Remember that managers receive anywhere from 5%-20% of the artist's gross or net income. Refer to page 35 to see the different ways artists are paid.

INFORMATION FOR ALL

Five ways to protect yourself in the business of music:

1. Own and control your copyrights
2. Own and control your music publishing
3. Own and control the rights, name, and likeness to your stage name and image (trademark & servicemark your stage name) Own and control your domain name i.e. www.yourstagename.com
4. Always have a competent music entertainment attorney review and draft your contracts.
5. Attempt not to sign long-term exclusive contracts; if you do, you better do number four.

When do I need a business license or tax I.D.?

When one wants to establish the business entity separate from the business owner they should apply for a business license and tax I.D. For instance, a personal checking account should be different from a business checking account.

How do I get a business license?

Normally, a business license may be obtained by contacting the local or county tax office. In most instances this information may be found either on the Internet or in the Local Yellow Pages.

What is a tax I.D.?

An EIN (Employer Identification Number) sometimes called a Federal Identification Number is used to identify business entities. If you are starting a Partnership, LLC (Limited Liability Company) or corporation you will need to apply for an EIN through the I.R.S. at www.irs.gov

How do I get a tax I.D.?

To obtain a tax I.D. (EIN/FIN) contact the I.R.S. at www.irg.gov. EIN's are free through the I.R.S.

What is the difference between a business license and a tax I.D.?

A business license grants you the right to legally do business in your city or county. A Federal Employer Identification Number (Tax I.D.) is used to identify your business entity with the I.R.S (Internal Revenue Service).

What is Dun & Bradstreet?

Dun & Bradstreet is a credit rating agency for businesses. In addition, Dun & Bradstreet tracks the credit worthiness of businesses much like Equifax, Experian and Transunion tracks the credit worthiness of individuals.

How may I contact Dun & Bradstreet?

- D&B Corporation, 103 JFK Parkway
  Short Hills, NJ 07078
  P) 800.234.3867
  custserv@dnb.com

Where may I get business cards printed for free?

Go to www.vistaprint.com to get free business cards.

How may I get flyers printed for free?

First, determine who may need to promote their business in the city. Remember the business does not necessarily have to be music related. For instance, a local clothing store, real estate agent or car dealership, may want to promote their business. Second, the business should be one that has the money, but not the time to distribute the flyers. Third, set up a meeting with the possible candidates. Fourth, let them know that you are an aspiring artist, producer, manager or engineer seeking a co-op (cooperative) opportunity to help spread the word about your businesses. Propose that they get one side of the flyer to promote their business and that you get the other to promote yours. Next propose that they pay for the printing of the flyers and that you distribute them. Inform them that because your business is promoted on one-side of the flyer that you have a “VESTED INTEREST” in insuring that the flyers are properly distributed. Remember to use the words “VESTED INTEREST” it has a very professional tone to it. Before you approach any one, remember that your typed proposal has the following details **the printing company you will be using, the exact price for printing, shipping and taxes if applicable, turnaround time (time it will take to get the flyers back) and your distribution points (drop-off locations).**

A number of my business associates have the money, but not the time to distribute flyers to promote their ventures. If you are willing to (do the leg work) distribute the flyers I may be able to get you started; for details contact me at either 800-963-0949 or jawar@mt101.com.

How may I get 50 to 100 Promotional CDs FREE?

You may either check the Local Sunday Newspaper or visit the websites of the following stores Best Buy, Circuit City, Staples, Office Max, and Office Depot for their rebate specials. Normally, **one of the stores will have a special offer where you may purchase anywhere from 50 to 100**

CD-Rs for free via their rebate program. Remember to keep your original receipt, barcode from the packaging and get the necessary rebate forms from the store.

All of the rebate specials are subject to certain terms, so ensure that you read all the fine print. For example, most of the programs are designed where you are only eligible (able) to get one rebate offer per person per household. In addition, there usually are expiration dates for the rebate programs.

Sometimes the rebate offers for CD-Rs may not be for free, but for a substantial discount. For instance, you may be able to purchase 50 CD-Rs for only $4.99 through the rebate program.

Once you have your blank CDs you simply need to burn (record) your music on them. Now you have anywhere from 50 to 100 promotional CDs. These may be used in your press kits, given away as promotional material or sold to fans.

Where may I use the Internet for FREE?

Most public libraries provide FREE Internet access. Some even offer access to Microsoft Word, Excel and PowerPoint for typing letters, invoices, proposals and presentations, etc. You will find that each library has its on way of doing things, so check around, find the one that works best for you and start using the Internet for FREE.

What is a One-Sheet?

A one-sheet is an industry standard document used to inform retailers, one-stops and distributors about a new release. A one-sheet contains the following:

- **CD Cover Artwork**
- **Barcode Number**
- **Suggested Retail Price**

- **Wholesale Price**
- **Record/Distributor Contact Details for Ordering product**
- **Special Artist Mention i.e. is there any platinum artists, writers or producers featured on the project, etc.**

What is a Split Sheet?

A split sheet is a document that shows who the writer(s), producer(s) and musician(s) are of a particular song. More importantly it easily identifies what percentage each person contributed to a song. A split sheet is a simple way to keep everyone involved in creating a song honest. Every recording studio, songwriter, producer, musician, manager and entertainment attorney should have a few copies on hand. Split sheets are included in the Music Therapy 101 Membership Kit. Details about the Music Therapy 101 Membership Program and how to enroll today may be found at the end of the book.

What is Soundexchange?

Soundexchange is responsible for collecting and distributing performance royalties in the digital media arena i.e. digital distribution, from such entities as webcasters, satellite radio and Internet radio service providers.

How do I contact Soundexchange?

- Soundexchange
  1330 Connecticut Ave. NW
  Suite 330 Washington, DC 20036
  P) 202.828.0120 F) 202.833.2141
  www.soundexchange.com

Where do Atlanta Music Industry Professionals network?

That really depends on the genre of music. However, you can normally find music professionals at Music

Conferences like Music Therapy 101, Music Festivals like the Sweet Auburn Festival, concerts sponsored by radio stations and strip clubs in Atlanta!

MUSIC RETAIL STORES

- Backstage Music
  7195-C Highway 85, Riverdale, GA 30274
  P) 770-996-5566

- Bambino's Music Store
  2521 Donald Lee Hollowell Pkwy, Suite B,
  Atlanta GA 30318
  P) 404-799-6060
  babinos@bellsouth.net

- Bernard's Records
  Attn: Leon Dockery
  3579 M.L. King Sr., Atlanta, GA 30031
  P) 404-699-0669

- Big Boy Records
  Contact: Johnny
  5002 Austell Rd., Austell, GA 30106
  P) 770-745-1909 Cell) 678-895-7623
  Bigboy_records@msn.com

- Big Oomp Records
  Attn: Store Promotions Dept.
  1079 MLK Drive NW, Ste 2, Atlanta, GA 30314

- Big Oomp Records
  1120 Ralph D. Abernathy, Suite 2, Atlanta, GA 30314
  P) 404-758-4210

- Big Oomp Records
  751 Simpson Rd., NW, Atlanta, GA 30314
  P) 404-223-6111

- Big Oomp Records
  1954 Candler Rd., Decatur, GA 30032
  P) 404-288-4007

- Big Oomp Records
  2925 Headland Dr., East Point, GA 30311
  P) 404-344-4711

- Big Oomp Records
  2668 Campbellton Rd., SW, Atlanta, GA 30311
  P) 404-349-0620

- Big Oomp Records
  813 Concord Rd., Smyrna, GA
  P) 770-436-7767

- Criminal Records
  466 Moreland Ave. Atlanta, GA 30307-1925
  P) 404-215-9511 F) 404-659-0320
  www.criminal.com

- Da Funk Shop
  Attn: Rick Fludd
  73 Peachtree Rd., Atlanta, GA 30303
  P) 404-525-7722 F) 404-525-9944
  dafunkshop@hotmail.com

- DBS Sounds
  5658 Riverdale Rd., Ste-P, College Park, GA 30349
  P) 770-997-5776
  www.dbssounds.com

- DBS Sounds:
  4841 Jonesboro Rd., Forest Park, GA 30297
  P) 404-366-9400

- Discolandia Record Shops (8)
  3352 Buford Hwy, Atlanta, GA 30329
  P) 404-417-0506

- Earwax Records
  565 Spring St., Atlanta, GA 30308
  P) 404-875-5600 F) 404-875-7393
  www.earwaxrecords.com
  earwax1@bellsouth.net

- Jay's Music
  Contact: Jason or Tanya
  880 New Hope Rd., Lawrenceville, GA 30045
  P) 770-338-0383 F) 770-338-0033

- Jumpstreet Records
  Contact: Xavier Baker
  5133 Old National Hwy, College Park, GA 30349
  P) 404-767-4844 F) 404-767-2993
  www.jumpstreetrecords.com
  ljumpin@aol.com

- Lady T's Records
  3897 Glenwood Rd., Decatur, GA
  P) 404-534-0744

- Major Turnout
  625 Lawrence St., Marietta, GA 30060
  P) 770-419-1526 F) 770-419-8544
  majorturnout@mindspring.com

- Midtown Music Room
  Contact: Victor D. Brown
  432 W. Solomon St., Griffin, GA 30223
  P) 770-233-1205

- Midtown Music Room
  Contact: Victor D. Brown
  Clayton Flea Market (D-3)
  867 Southway Dr., Jonesboro, GA 30236
  P) 770-374-0933

- Mo' Music
  Contact: Reggie Regg
  790 Cascade Ave., Atlanta, GA 30310
  P) 404-755-8050
  www.momusicent.com

- Mo' Music
  2234 S. Cobb Dr., Smyrna, GA 30080
  P) 678-556-9223
  www.momusicent.com

- Moods Music
  Contact: Darryl "D-Nice" Harris
  1130 Euclid Ave., Little 5 Points, Atlanta, GA 30307
  P) 404-653-0724
  www.moodsmusic.net
  info@moodsmusic.net

- More Dusty Than Digital
  1139 Euclid Ave., Atlanta, GA 30307
  P) 404-577-5855 F) 404-577-5895
  www.moredusty.com

- Music Media
  2701 Candler Rd., Decatur, GA 30024
  P) 404-381-0024

- Music Vibrations
  Attn: Nina Baddie Smith
  822 McDonough Blvd., Atlanta, GA 30315
  P) 404-633-1562 F) 404-635-1542
  P) 404-635-1562

- North GA Compact Disc
  Attn: Michelle Ceawright
  515 Beaver Ruin Rd., Norcross, GA 30071
  P) 770-416-6575

- Peppermint Records (3)

West End Mall, 819 Oak St., SW, Atlanta, GA
P) 404-572-9494

- Rebel Musik: (2)
  353 Edgewood Ave., Atlanta, GA 30312
  P) 404-584-0780

- Satellite Records
  Contact: Greg Adamson
  421 Moreland Ave., Atlanta, GA 30307
  P) 404-880-9746 F) 404-880-0350
  www.satelliterecords.com
  greg@satelliterecords.com

- Super Sound Music
  2740 Greenbriar Pkwy. SW, Suite #9,
  Atlanta, GA 30331
  P) 404-349-2969

- Super Sounds Music
  4919 Flatshoals Parkway, Suite 108, Decatur, GA 30034
  P) 770-323-5720 F) 770-323-5279

- Super Sound Music
  79 Price Quarters Rd., McDonough, GA
  P) 678-556-9223

- Third World Enterprises
  2091 Candler Rd., Decatur, GA 30032

- Time for CD
  3579 Martin Luther King Dr., Atlanta, GA
  P) 404-699-0669

- Top 20 Records
  Contact: Michael Cohen
  2524 Bouldercrest Rd., Suite B, Atlanta, GA
  P) 404-241-1230 Cell) 404-538-3235

- Top 20 Records
  Contact: Michael Cohen
  2751 Donald Lee Howell Pkwy, Atlanta, GA 30318
  P) 404-794-9600 F) 404-794-9133 Cell) 404-538-3235

- Tower Records
  3232 Peachtree Rd., Atlanta, GA 30305
  Contact: Consignment Coordinator, Missy Wright
  P) 404-264-1217
  www.tower.com

- Turn It Up Records
  3752 Cascade Rd., Suite #130 Atlanta, GA 30311
  P) 404-699-0056

- Vibes Music & More
  Attn: J Warren
  145-B Sycamore St., Decatur, GA 30030
  P) 404-373-5099

- Wax N' Facts
  432 Moreland Ave., NE, Atlanta, GA
  P) 404-525-2275

- World Wide Music
  Contact: Reginald "Motsi Ski" Abrams
  5540 Old National Hwy., College Park, GA 30349
  P) 404-209-1823

- World Wide Music
  961 Point South Parkway, Jonesboro, GA
  P) 678-216-0300

COLLEGE & COMMUNITY RADIO

College and Community Radio Stations tend to be more receptive to playing independent or underground music. For this reason it may be of greater benefit to solicit your music to these stations before attempting to get radio airplay from commercial radio stations. In addition, these stations are usually open to an artist scheduling an on-air interview, providing drops or leaving music to be given away to station listeners. All these opportunities should be explored to help increase an artist's fan base and generate more sales.

- 88.5 WRAS-Format All
  MSC 8L0377
  Georgia State University, 33 Gilmer St., SE, Unit 8,
  Atlanta, GA 30303
  Office 404-651-2240 DJ 404-651-4488

- 89.3 WRFG Radio Free Georgia-Format All
  1083 Austin Ave. NE, Atlanta, GA 30307-1940
  P) 404-523-3471 Request Line) 404-523-8989
  www.wrfg.org
  info@wrfg.org

- 91.1 WREK-Format All
  Georgia Tech
  165 Eighth St NW, Atlanta, GA 30332
  P) 404-894-2468 F) 404-894-6872
  www.wrek.org

- 91.9 WCLK Clark Atlanta University
  111 James P. Brawley St., SW, Atlanta, GA 30314
  P) 404-880-8273 Request Line) 404-880-9255

- WRME -Format All
  PO Drawer AG, Atlanta, GA 30322
  Emory University
  P) 404-727-9672 F) 404-712-8000 Request Line

404-727-9673
www.wmre.org

COMMERICAL RADIO

Contrary to popular belief commercial radio should be the last stop an artist should approach for marketing a new release. Normally, an artist will need deep pockets **($$$)** and the right contacts to get any significant radio airplay. For these reasons artist should continue to perfect their craft, grow a loyal fan base and perform every chance they get. After successfully doing this, you may want to retain (hire and/or secure) the services of a professional radio promotions consultant. Traditionally, a radio promotions consultant, artist and/or label would have a series of meetings with the radio station program/music director in an effort to get a new song played and possibly added to the stations rotation. Below is a list of Atlanta area commercial radio stations.

- 1160AM WMLB-Adult Contemporary
  130 M.L. King Jr. Dr., SE, Atlanta, GA 30312
  P) 404-681-9307 F) 404-659-1329

- 1340AM WALR-Gospel
  3535 Piedmont Rd. Bldg.14, Suite 1200, Atlanta, GA 30305
  P) 404-688-0068 F) 404-995-4045

- 1380AM WAOK-Gospel
  1201 W. Peachtree St NW, Ste 800, Atlanta, GA 30309
  P) 404-898-8900 F) 404-898-8987

- 1480AM WYZE-Gospel
  1111 Boulevard SE, Atlanta, GA 30312
  P) 404-622-7802 F) 404-622-6767

- 92.9FM WZGC-Rock
  1100 Johnson Ferry Rd NE, Suite 593,

Atlanta, GA 30342
P) 404-851-9393 F) 404-843-3541

- 94.1FM WSTR-Hispanic
  3350 Peachtree Rd NE, Suite 1800, Atlanta, GA 30326
  P) 404-261-2970 F) 404-365-9026

- 94.9FM WPCH- Adult Contemporary
  1819 Peachtree Rd NE Suite 700, Atlanta, GA 30309
  P) 404-367-0949 F) 404-367-9490

- 96.1FM WKLS-Rock
  1819 Peachtree Rd NE Suite 700, Atlanta, GA 30309
  P) 404-325-0960 F) 404-367-1156

- 97.5FM WPZE-Urban
  75 Piedmont Ave SE, Atlanta, GA 30303
  P) 404-765-9750

- 99.7FM WNNX-Rock
  780 Johnson Ferry Rd NE, Atlanta, GA 30342
  P) 404-266-0997 F) 404-364-5855

- 100.5FM WWWQ-Top 40
  780 Johnson Ferry Rd, NE, Atlanta, GA 30342
  P) 404-497-4700 F) 404-364-5855

- 101.5FM WKHX-Country
  210 Interstate North Pkwy SE FL 6, Atlanta, GA 30339
  P) 770-955-0101 F) 770-850-0101

- 102.5FM WAMJ-Old/Urban
  75 Piedmont Ave, 10th FL, Atlanta, GA 30303
  P) 404-765-9750 F) 404-688-7686

- 103.3FM WVEE-Urban/R&B
  1201 W. Peachtree St. NW, Suite 800,
  Atlanta, GA 30309
  P) 404-898-8900 F) 404-898-8987

- 104.1FM WALR-R&B
  1601 W. Peachtree St. NE, Atlanta, GA 30309
  P) 404-897-7500 F) 404-897-6595

- 107.5FM WJZZ-Jazz
  75 Piedmont Ave., Atlanta, GA 30303
  P) 404-765-9750 F) 404-688-7686

- 107.9FM WHAT-Urban
  75 Piedmont Ave 10th FL, Atlanta, GA 30303
  P) 404-765-9750 F) 404-688-7686

INTERNET RADIO STATIONS

- www.atlanta11.com/radio.htm
- www.atlantabluesky.com - Blues
- www.digital-djs.com
- www.dr-love.com - Hip Hop, R&B, Neo-Soul
- www.dryerbuzz.com - Hip Hop, R&B, Neo-Soul
- www.liquidsoulradio.com - Neo-Soul, R&B
- www.urbanindiemusic.com- Hip Hop, R&B, Neo-Soul
- www.xmradio.com - All
- www.web-radio.fm - Locate radio stations

MUSIC MAGAZINES

- BRE (Black Radio Exclusive)
  Contact: Carol U. Ozemhoya
  903 Calibre Springs Way, N.E., Atlanta, GA 30342
  P) 404-843-3208 F) 404-843-2714
  www.bremagazine.com
  brecarol@aol.com

- Crunk
  Contact: Desmick Perkins
  1744 Alvarado Terrace, Atlanta, GA 30310
  P) 404-756-986 F) 404-756-0494
  www.crunkmag.com

desmick@crunckmag.com

- Entouch Magazine
  Contact: G.M. Hamilton
  1970 Cliff Valley Way, Suite 250, Atlanta, GA 30329
  P) 404-320-5212 F) 404-320-5214
  www.entouchmag.com

- GA Up & Coming
  Contact: Sean Stanley
  P.O. Box 6673, Macon, GA 31213
  P) 478-736-1105
  Gaupandcomingmag3000@yahoo.com

- Hip Hop Encounter
  P.O. Box 1133, Experiment, GA 30212
  www.hiphopencounter.com

- Holla
  P.O. Box 1367, Smyrna, GA 30081
  945 Windy Hill Rd., Smyrna, GA 30081
  P) 770-438-0112 F) 770-438-1228
  www.hollamag.com

- Industry Status
  P.O. Box 1578, Roswell, GA 30077
  P) 770-640-1271 F) 770-650-9825
  www.industrystatus.com
  sales@industrystatus.com

- Look Magazine
  Contact: Rodney Jones
  3915 Cascade Rd., Suite T-115, Atlanta, GA 30331
  P) 404-696-4034 Cell) 404-438-5158
  www.lookmag.com
  rjones@lookmag.com

- **THE MIC (Music Industry Connection)**
  P.O. Box 52682, Atlanta, GA 30355
  Toll-Free 800-963-0949

- NEO Entertainment Magazine
  2451 Cumberland Pkwy, Suite 3529, Atlanta, GA 30339
  P) 770-256-2947

- Southeast Performer
  449 ½ Moreland Ave. #206, Atlanta, GA 30307
  P) 404-582-0088 F) 404-582-0089
  www.performermag.com
  sepeditortial@performermag.com

- Stomp & Stammer
  P.O. Box 55233, Atlanta, GA 30308
  P) 706-369-0833 F) 706-369-0218
  www.stompandstammer.com
  mailroom@stompandstammer.com

- WETS (We The Streets)
  Contact: JaWar or Ray
  5319 Old National Hwy., College Park, GA 30349
  P) 404-684-5999

How To Use Record Pools To Test-Market Your Next Hit

Record pools are DJ Membership organizations that give you cost-effective access to radio, club and mobile DJs. Essentially, DJs pay either a monthly, quarterly or yearly dues to be a record pool member. In exchange for paying membership dues the record pool distributes new music to the DJs in either CD or Vinyl Formats. Normally, the DJs are required to give feedback or listener response to the pool director in a timely fashion. For instance, the DJs may report to the pool director once a week. When the DJs have sent in their feedback reports the pool director compiles a chart list that is distributed to record companies via fax and/or email. The chart list is sent regularly. For instance, it may be sent once a week or twice a month. Record pools are one of the most cost-effective ways to either generate a buzz or monitor a potential hit. It should be noted that record pools tend to work best for styles of music that are played in clubs i.e. Dance, Hip Hop R&B, Pop and Trip Hop, etc. One of the reasons that there may be a Club or Dance Remix to a song is so it may be played in a nightclub setting.

Many record pools have regular meetings either bi-weekly, monthly or quarterly. Actively attending these meetings is a fantastic way to meet the DJs that can help break your record. By actively participating I mean attending these meetings prepared to network. For instance, make sure that you have business cards, flyers and other promotional material to distribute to everyone at the meeting. I attended the Legion of Doom Record Pool Meeting in Atlanta and was able to give a few copies of my newspaper the **MIC (Music Industry Connection)** to Greg Street. Greg is one of the top radio-personalities in Atlanta, Georgia and Dallas, Texas yet he was very approachable during the meeting. Because record pool meetings are music business events most people are receptive to networking. It has been my experience that record pool meetings are some of the best places to meet industry tastemakers in your own backyard. In addition to networking with industry tastemakers in your own backyard, record pool meetings are an excellent way to get immediate response from DJs about your new music. DJs tend to be very honest when giving feedback about new music at these events. Some of the record pool meetings offer live talent showcases for artists to perform in. While sponsorship (paying money) is normally required to perform in the record pool talent showcases it usually is worth the investment to perform in front of the DJs that can help propel your career. **Remember to treat everyone that you meet like they are the most important person on earth.** Not only will this move your career forward faster, but more importantly it will help you have more fun in a cutthroat industry. In addition, you never know whom you may be talking to; it could be a radio station music/program director or editor of a music magazine. This is especially true when you begin attending record pool meetings outside your home market.

Now, let's say that you are an independent record company in Atlanta, Georgia and you're preparing to release a CD. Before spending all your advertising dollars in Atlanta, you will want to test-market your first single using record pools in Georgia, Alabama, South Carolina and Florida. After a few weeks you might find that your single is getting a so-so response in Atlanta, but in Birmingham, Alabama and South Carolina your single has the potential of being this year's summer hit! Since, Birmingham and South Carolina are only a two and three hour drive from Atlanta, respectively, it might make good sense to spend more of your advertising dollars in those areas, remember the How to Promote Your Independent Release Article in the first chapter. This will increase your opportunities for creating a street buzz faster and turning a profit sooner via CD, concert ticket and merchandising sales.

Before spending you hard earned money from your day job pursuing your music career at night, consider record pools as a cost-effective method of test-marketing your next hit. At the end of this book are details on obtaining record pool names, the pool director, the physical mailing address, phone & fax number, website and email address if applicable. The record pool list is available in both a print and CD E-Book version. The CD version is great, because it allows you to quickly find record pools across the U.S. either by name or by state and is compatible with Microsoft Excel for PCs. You may order your list of over 130 U.S. Record Pools by completing and mailing in the order-form at the end of this book. Reprint courtesy of JaWar and Music Industry Connection, LLC.

RECORD POOLS

- Atlanta Star Record Pool
  Contact: Marvin Howard
  7435 Crescent Bend Cove, Stone Mountain, GA 30087
  P) 770-498-2795 F) 770-498-4461
  Atlantastar2000@yahoo.com

- Dixie Dance Kings Record Pool
  Contact: Dan Miller
  42 Milton Ave., Alpharetta, GA 30004
  P) 770-740-9067 F) 770-740-0358

- Legion of Doom Record Pool
  Contact: Ray Hamilton
  5319 Old National Highway, College Park, GA 30349
  P) 404-684-5898 P) 404-392-9415
  F) 404-684-5973
  thelegionofdoomdjs@yahooo.com

- Million Dollar Record Pool
  2459 Roosevelt Hwy., Suite B-1,
  College Park, GA 30337
  P) 404-766-1275

mde@mildol.com

How are CD sales tracked?

CDs sold through music retail stores are normally tracked by SoundScan. A CD must contain a U.P.C. Barcode, must be registered with SoundScan and the retail store must be a SoundScan reporting store before the CD will be tracked through the SoundScan System.

How do I ensure proper credit for my CD sales?

- Contact SoundScan Client Services
  One North Lexington Avenue, Gateway Building, 14 FL
  White Plains, NY 10601
  P) 914-684-5525 F) 914-684-5606
  www.soundscan.com

Does SoundScan also track CDs sold at live performances?

Yes, SoundScan tracks CDs sold at live performances.

To track CDs sold at live performances contact:

- SoundScan Venue Service
  P) 914-684-5506 F) 914-686-1556
  www.soundscan.com

Who tracks and monitors radio airplay?

BDS and Mediabase track radio airplay. Registering a song with BDS and/or Mediabase is important to determine the correct number of spins or times a song is played on commercial radio to insure accurate chart position i.e. Billboard Charts. It should be noted that ASCAP, BMI and SESAC also monitor radio airplay to ensure that their writers and publishers are paid public performance royalties (money).

BDS and Mediabase may be contacted at the following:

- BDS (Broadcast Data Service)
  550 11th St., Suite 201, Miami Beach, FL 33139
  P) 305-777-2371 F) 305-777-2372
  www.bdsonline.com

- Mediabase
  P) 818-377-5300
  www.mediabase.com

PROMOTERS

- Coming Attractions Promotions
  Contact: Arlinda Garrett
  2375 Wesley Chapel Rd., Suite 3-1118,
  Decatur, GA 30035
  P) 404-886-4650
  arlindamay@aol.com

- Doug Craig
  Attn: Universal
  P) 678-421-0310

- Dulo Marketing & Media
  Attn: Kaspa
  1440 Dutch Valley Place, Suite 950, Atlanta, GA 30324
  P) 404-607-8755 C) 404-202-6232
  pleeziwana@aol.com

- Glo Hunter
  Specializes in National Retail Promotions
  208 Vinings Forest Circle, Smyrna, GA 30380
  P) 770-436-7459

- High Profile Music
  Contact: CityLites
  P.O. Box 90364, Atlanta, GA 30364-0364
  P) 404-572-9177

highprofilemusic@yahoo.com

- Jerome Marketing & Promotions
  Contact: Billy Jerome
  2535 Winthrope Way, Lawrenceville, GA 30044
  P) 770-982-7055 F) 770-982-1882
  www.jeromepromotions.com

- New Step Promotions
  989 Pointer Ridge, Tucker, GA 30084
  P) 404-755-0114 P) 678-596-7015
  www.newsteppromotions.com
  newsteppromo@yahoo.com

- Party Promotions
  Contact: Donald Jarmond
  4470 Riders Ridge Trail, Suite 114,
  Snellville, GA 30039
  P) 770-609-2877 F) 678-344-8403 Cell) 678-595-0938
  www.partypromotions.com
  djarmond@partypromotions.com

- Real Street Promotions
  Contact: Real
  1440 Dutch Valley Place, Atlanta, GA 30324, Suite 700
  P) 404-685-8996 F) 404-685-1678
  www.realstreetpromo.com
  info@realstreetpromo.com

- Silent Note
  Contact: Danny Pearson
  5156 Affton Way SE, Smyrna, GA 30080
  P) 770-521-8558
  www.silentnote.com

- Sixthman
  83 Walton Street, 4th Floor, Atlanta, GA 30303
  P) 404-525-0222
  www.sixthman.net

- T.R.Y Marketing
  Contact: Tanya
  P.O. Box 464635, Lawrenceville, GA 30042
  P) 404-273-7135

- Urban Icon Lifestyle Marketing
  Contact: Rob Webb
  1009 Oak Chase Dr., Suite P, Tucker, GA 30084
  P) 770-908-8532

- Vintage Imperial
  Contact: Kid Kaos
  P) 404-734-8499
  www.vintageimperial.com
  kidkaos@illverb.com

MUSIC BUSINESS BOOKS

- 100 Miles To A Record Deal
  by Bronson Herrmuth
  www.iowahomegown.com

- Everything You'd Better Know About the Recording Industry By Kashif
  kashif@pacificnet.net

- How to Get Paid from the Record Game
  By Raheem
  P) 678-508-3897
  Rah4life@bellsouth.net
  www.tight2defrecords.com

- Making It In The Music Business: The Insider Secretes
  By Campbell, Waters, Allen

- Official Contact Pages to the Music Business
  www.musiccontactpages.com
- The Record Game Can Be a Dirty Game
  By Raheem

P) 678-508-3897
Rah4life@bellsouth.net
www.tight2defrecords.com

- Urban Music Industry Contacts
  By Ty Young
  www.recorddeals.net

INTERNET RESOURCE GUIDE

- Atlantamusicguide.com
- Atlantamusician.com
- Atlantashows.org
- Georgiabands.com
- Slabmusic.com
- Wholeteam.com

GRAPHIC DESIGN COMPANIES

- Alexxus Graphics
  625 Lawrence St., Marietta, GA 30060
  P) 770-419-1526 F) 770-419-8544

- Blaze 1 Graphixs
  Contact: Gordon Mills
  4548 Howell Farms Rd., Ackworth, GA 30303
  P) 770-975-0522
  www.blaze1graphixs.com

- Creative Juice
  6303 Chastain Drive NE, Atlanta, GA 30342
  P) 404-851-1685 F) 404-851-1684
  dvsjuice@aol.com

- Eboni Graphix
  Contact: Leticia R. Beverly
  3350 Riverwood Parkway, Suite 1900,
  Atlanta, GA 30339

P) 678-354-9078 F) 678-354-3997
www.eboni-graphix.com
lbeverly@eboni-graphix.com

- Green Designs
  Contact: Trevor D. Green
  5744 Norman Ct., College Park, GA 30349
  P) 404-388-6888 F) 770-991-0120
  www.greendesigns.org
  tgreen@greendesigns.org

- I Design Graphics
  4600 Cascade Rd., Atlanta, GA 30331
  P) 404-505-1443 F) 404-691-5209
  www.ithanpaynecreative.com
  ithanpayne@aol.com

- Jamire
  P.O. Box 492494, College Park, GA 30349
  P) 866-629-3475 P) 404-403-2729
  www.jamire.com
  tcarpenter@jamire.com

- Mastermind Graphics
  www.mm-graphics.com
  P) 866-529-4664 P) 404-529-9937
  F) 404-529-5538
  contact@mm-graphics.com

- Moz Graphics
  4120 Jeffrey Dr., College Park, GA 30349
  P) 404-849-3220
  www.mozgraphics.com

- New World Group
  Contact: John Wallace
  1117 Peachtree Walk, Suite 123, Atlanta, GA 30309
  P) 404-876-6366
  www.nwgsite.com

- **Next Level Entertainment**
  Contact: Derick Leslie
  1508 Crooked Tree Lane, Stone Mountain, GA 30088
  P) 404-578-2653
  Deesn14@yahoo.com

- One 3 Creative
  565 Dutch Valley Rd., Atlanta, GA 30324
  P) 404-872-30324

- Star Shooters Atlanta
  277-B East Paces Ferry Rd, Atlanta, GA 30305
  P) 404-869-8844 F) 404-869-8833

MUSIC CONSULTANTS

- A&R Music1.com, LLC
  Contact: Stephen Strother
  2132 Sara Ashley Way - Suite 300 Lithonia, GA 30058
  P) 770-686-9100 x727

- Music Business Consultants
  Contact: Ty Young
  2020 Howell Mill Rd., Suite C-102, Atlanta, GA 30318
  P) 404-586-0037 F) 404-815-0668
  www.recorddeals.net
  musicbizchic@aol.com

- **Music Industry Connection**
  P.O. Box 52682, Atlanta, GA 30355
  P) 800-963-0949
  www.mt101.com
  questions@mt101.com

- Music Q & A
  www.musicqanda.com

- Right Path Industry Consultants
  8622 Glendevon Ct., Riverdale, GA 30274
  Contact: Carl Schackleton
  P) 404-427-0477 F) 770-471-0825
  www.rightpathconsultant.com
  Carl@rightpathconsultant.com

- Seven Diamond Foundation
  P.O. Box 16806, Atlanta, GA 30321
  P) 770-572-0700 P) 404-899-3299
  www.startyourrecordlabel.com
  Se7en@startyourrecordlabel.com

- Xavier Entertainment
  Contact: Mose Hardin
  6980 Roswell Rd., D-11, Atlanta, GA 30328
  P) 678-984-5882
  www.xavierentertainment.net

MUSIC ORGANIZATIONS

- AFM-Atlanta Federation of Musicians
  551 Dutch Valley Road NE, Atlanta, GA 30324
  P) 800-854-5178 P) 404-873-2033 F) 404-873-0019
  www.atlantamusicians.com

- ASCAP-American Society of Composers, Authors and Publishers
  541 Tenth St. NW, #PMB 500, Atlanta, GA 30318
  P) 404-351-1224 F) 404-351-1252
  www.ascap.com

- BMI-Broadcast Music, Inc.
  P.O. Box 19199, Atlanta, GA 31126
  P) 404-261-5151 F) 404-261-5152
  www.bmi.com

- GMIA-Georgia Music Industry Association
  3063 Clairmont Rd. NE, Atlanta, Georgia 30329
  P) 404-633-7772
  www.gmia.org

- NARAS -National Academy of Recording Arts and Sciences
  (Grammy's) Atlanta Chapter
  3290 Northside Parkway, Suite 280, Atlanta, GA 30327
  P) 404-816-1380 F) 404-816-1390
  www.grammy.com
  Atlanta@grammy.com

- SECUR-Southeast Coalition of Urban Retailers
  Contact: Monique Smith
  1188 Richard Rd., Decatur, GA 30032
  P) 404-288-1590

- SOFRAS-Society of Future Recording Artists & Songwriters
  P.O. Box 930274, Norcross, GA 30003-0274
  P) 770-281-7286 P/F) 866-442-1926
  www.sofras.net

ENTERTAINMENT ATTORNEYS

- Alston & Bird, LLP
  Contact: Cherri T. Gregg
  One Atlantic Center
  1201 West Peachtree Street, Atlanta, GA 30309
  P) 404-881-4953 P) 404-881-7000 F) 404-253-8444
  www.alston.com
  cgreeg@alston.com

- Brison & Associates, LLC
  2100 DeFoors Ferry Rd., #2025, Atlanta, GA 30318
  P) 404-931-3391
  nbrison@comcast.net

- Brock, Clay, Wilson & Rogers
  49 Atlanta St., Marietta, GA 30060
  P) 770-422-1776
  www.bccwr.com

- Charles J. Driebe Jr.
  6 Courthouse Wy, Jonesboro, GA 30236
  P) 770-478-8894 F) 770-478-9606

- Clarke & Anderson
  3355 Lenox Rd., Suite 750, Atlanta, GA 30326-1332
  P) 404-816-9800 F) 404-816-0555

- Cohen, Cooper, Estep & Mudder, LLC
  3350 Riverwood Parkway, Suite 2220,
  Atlanta, GA 30339
  P) 404-814-0000 F) 404-816-8900
  www.coco-law.tv

- David & Baldwin LLC
  P) 404-529-9300

- Drew, Esq.
  568 14th St., NW, Suite 100, Atlanta, GA 30318

P) 404-876-4636

- Drew M. Jackson
  P) 404-609-9885

- Ewing & Roseberry
  1741 Commerce Dr., Atlanta, GA 30318
  P) 404-352-0404 F) 404-352-0405
  monicaewingesq@mindspring.com

- Georgia Lawyers for the Arts
  675 Ponce de Leon Ave, NE, Atlanta, GA 30308
  P) 404-873-3911
  gla@glarts.org

- Greenberg Trauriq Atlanta, LLP
  The Forum
  3290 Northside Pkwy., Suite 400, Atlanta, GA 30327
  P) 678-553-2100 F) 678-553-2212

- H. Oliver Welch
  1417 Wesley Walk NW, Atlanta, GA 30327-1711
  P) 404-351-8408 F) 404-873-1224

- Hewitt, Katz, Stepp & Wright
  Contact: Leron E. Rogers
  Resurgens Plaza, Suite 2610
  945 East Paces Ferry Road, Atlanta, GA 30326
  P) 404-240-0400 F) 404-240-0401
  lrogers@atlantalawofc.com

- Holland & Knight LLP
  One Atlantic Center
  1201 W. Peachtree St., NE, Suite 2000, Atlanta, GA 30309
  P) 404-817-8500 F) 404-881-0470

- Hudson & Associates P.C.
  P.O. Box 7929, Atlanta, GA 30357

P) 404-897-5252 F) 404-897-5677
www.arts-entertainmentlaw.com
Hudson@arts-entertainmentlaw.com

- **John F. Christmas Entertainment & Sports Attorney**
  P.O. Box 615, Union City, GA 30291
  P) 770-374-8294 F) 770-306-0664
  jochristm@aol.com

- Katz, Smith & Cohen
  3290 Northside Dr., Suite 400, Atlanta, GA 30327
  P) 404-237-7700 P) 678-553-2100 F) 678-553-2212
  www.gtlaw.com

- Law Offices of Dale Richardson
  Contact: Dale Richardson
  P.O. Box 13828, Atlanta, GA 30324
  P) 404-812-1699
  www.law-offices-of-richardson.com
  dale_Richardson@bellsouth.net

- Law Office of Kendall A. Minter
  Contact: Joseph Arrington, II, Esq.
  5398 East Mountain St.,
  Stone Mountain, GA 30083-3079
  P) 770-879-7400 F) 770-879-5695
  jarringtonll@hotmail.com

- Lopes McKamey-Lopes
  44 Broad St., NW, Suite 504, Atlanta, GA 30303-0060
  P) 404-589-9000 F) 404-832-4120
  firm@lopesmckameylopes.com

- Marvin S. Harrington, Jr.
  P) 404-633-3396

- Moore & Hawton
  P) 404-524-2415

- Neighbors, Lett & Johnson, LLC
  Contact: J. Martin Lett
  The Candler Building
  127 Peachtree St., Suite 555, Atlanta, GA 30303
  P) 404-653-0881 F) 404-653-1171
  www.neighborslettandjohnson.com
  jlett@neighborslettandjohnson.com

- Rob Hassett
  990 Hammond Dr., Suite 990, Atlanta, GA 30328
  P) 770-393-0990 F) 770-901-9417
  www.internetlegal.com
  rob@internetlegal.com

- Robinson & Morgan
  3355 Peachtree Rd., Suite 500, Atlanta, GA 30326
  P) 404-995-7060 F) 404-995-7001

- Scott D. Sanders P.C.
  1252 W. Peachtree St., NW, Suite 500,
  Atlanta, GA 30309
  P) 404-874-6262

- Self, Glass & Davis
  The Platinum Tower
  400 Interstate North Pkwy, Suite 1650,
  Atlanta, GA 30339
  P) 770-563-9300 F) 770-563-9330
  ejb@sgdlaw.com

- Sharon M. Chavis
  2368 Ridgecrest Lane, East Point, GA 30344-2143
  P) 404-767-5522 F) 404-761-7487

- Shuli L. Green
  P.O. Box 2839, Decatur, GA 30031-2839
  P) 404-222-8411
  shuligreen@yahoo.com

- Standford, Fagant & Giolito
  1401 Peachtree St., NE, Suite 238, Atlanta, GA 30309
  P) 404-897-1000 F) 404-897-1990

- Stephanie S. Kika
  8108 Trolley Sqxing NE, Atlanta, GA 30306-5201
  P) 770-664-9262 F) 770-892-2150

- Stokes & Murphy
  3593 Hemphill St., Atlanta, GA 30337-0468
  P) 404-766-0076 F) 404-766-0076
  mail@stokesnmurphy.com

- Vernon Slaughter
  1741 Commerce Drive, Atlanta, GA 30318
  P) 404-355-2755 F) 404-355-2720
  slaughterv@bellsouth.net

- Vince Phillips
  P.O. Box 20084, Atlanta GA 30325
  P) 404-522-8000 F) 404-522-7643

- Washington Law Firm
  Contact: Karl Washington
  1353 Cleveland, East Point, GA 30344
  P) 404-768-3963 F) 404-768-3966
  karlwashington@att.net

- Weiznecker, Rose, Mattern & Fisher, P.C.
  1800 Peachtree Street, NW, Suite 620,
  Atlanta, GA 30309
  P) 404-365-9799 F) 404-917-0979
  www.wrmflaw.com

VIDEO PRODUCTION COMPANIES

- A Town Filmworks
  Contact: Ray Culpepper
  6803 Yorkdale Court, Lithonia, GA 30058
  P) 770-484-1644 F) 770-484-1844
  www.a-townfilmworks.com
  ray@a-townfilmworks.com

- Antone Productions Services
  644 Antone St., Atlanta, GA 30318
  P) 404-351-3211 F) 404-355-2287

- Bussey Video Productions
  3120 Perch Overlook, Marietta, GA 30008
  P) 770-439-5235
  www.busseyvideoproductions.com
  busseyideo@aol.com

- Chez Creative, Inc.
  Contact: Deborah E. Harrison
  3588 Hwy. 138 S.E., #266, Stockbridge, GA 30281
  P) 770-478-6226 F) 770-478-8845
  Chez1c@aol.com

- Cut Close Production
  Contact: Tray
  P) 678-570-8900

- Devine Communications
  1201 Peachtree Bldg-400, Suite 200, Atlanta, GA 30361
  P) 404-870-9125 F) 404-870-9005

- EMB Filmworks
  Contact: Edford M. Banuel
  1962 Spectrum Circle, Suite 260,
  Marietta, GA 30067
  P) 770-514-1406
  emfilmworks@aol.com

- Folks Creative
  Contact: Jada Harris
  4249 Courtside Dr., Stone Mountain, GA 30083
  P) 404-932-5760
  jadarenee@yahoo.com

- Global Eye Films
  P) 404-386-5996

- Guerilla le Femme Productions
  Contact: Demetria Clark
  Cell) 404-819-6976 Studio) 404-222-9547
  demetria@tmail.com

- IXL Film & Video
  1888 Emery St., NW, Atlanta, GA
  404-267-7600

- Magic Eye Productions
  193 Taft St., SW, Atlanta, GA 30315
  magiceye@bellsouth.net

- Motley Motion Films
  Contact: Fran Strine
  678-754-2510
  www.motelymotion.com
  fran@motleymotion.com

- Quiver Mill Pictures
  P) 404-355-7468

- Real 2 Real Studios
  7815 Old Morrow Rd., Jonesboro, GA 30236
  P) 770-472-4747 F) 770-472-2371

- R.V. & R Video Productions
  P.O. Box 371737, Atlanta, GA 30037
  P) 404-241-4191
  www.rvrvideoproductions.com

- Sky
  6849 Sandy Creek Dr., Riverdale, GA 30274
  P) 770-909-9213 C) 404-693-7860
  elthe3rd@yahoo.com

- Tag Image Productions
  690 Fairburn Rd., Atlanta, GA 30311
  P) 404-228-6917

- Victoria Productions
  Contact: Victoria Williams-Bryant
  835 Ashley Laine Walk, Lawrenceville, GA 30043
  P) 770-339-1060
  www.thepwg.com/victoriaproductions

ATLANTA CLUBS & VENUES

Apache Café
64 3rd St., NW, Atlanta, GA 30308
P) 404-876-5436

Andres Upstairs
56 East Andres Drive, Suite 13, Atlanta, GA 30305
P) 404-467-1600

Café 290
290 Hildebrand Rd., Atlanta, GA
P) 404-256-3942

Callanwolde Fine Arts Center
980 Briarcliff Rd., Atlanta, GA
P) 404-872-5338

Carnival
210 Pharr Rd., Buckhead, GA
P) 404-261-8476

Chastain Park Amphitheatre
4469 Stella Dr, Sandy Springs, GA
P) 404-733-4800

Club 1150
1150 Peachtree St., Atlanta, GA

Cotton Club
152 Luckie St, Atlanta, GA
P) 404-688-1193

Crescent Room
1136 Crescent Ave, Midtown, GA
P) 404-875-5252

Deux Plex

1789 Cheshire Bridge Rd, Buckhead, GA
P) 404-733-5900

Earthlink Live
1374 West Peachtree St, Midtown, Atlanta, GA
P) 404-885-1365

Echo Lounge
551 Flat Shoals Ave, East Atlanta Village, GA
P) 440-681-3600

Eleven 50
1150 b Peachtree St, Atlanta
P) 404-874-0428

Endenu Restaurant
393 Marietta St, Atlanta, GA
P) 404-522-8874

Ferst Center of The Arts
349 Ferst Dr, Atlanta, GA
P) 404-894-9600

Hifi Buys Amphitheatre
2002 Lakewood Way, SW Atlanta, GA
P) 404-443-5090

House of Blues
1374 West Peachtree St, Atlanta, GA
P) 404-885-1163

MJQ Concourse
736 Ponce De Leon Ave, Midtown, GA
P) 404-870-0575

Northside Tavern
1058 Howell Mill Rd, Atlanta, GA,
P) 404-874-8745

Smiths Olde Bar
1578 Piedmont Ave. Atlanta, GA, 30324
P) 404-875-1522

The Arena, the Gwinnett Center
1775 Pleasant Hill Rd @ Crestwood, Duluth GA 30096
P) 770-923-1775

The Atrium
5479 Memorial Dr, Stone Mountain, GA

The Fox Theatre
600 Peachtree St, Atlanta, GA
P) 404-249-6400

The Liquid Lounge
1355 Roswell Rd, Marietta, GA
P) 678-285-0538

The Masquerade
695 North Ave, Atlanta, GA
P) 404-577-8178

The Roxy
3110 Roswell Rd, Atlanta, GA
P) 404-233-ROXY

The Tabernacle
152 Luckie St, Atlanta, GA
P) 404-659-9022

Variety Playhouse
1099 Euclid Ave, Little 5 Points
Atlanta

Visionz
Peachtree Rd., Atlanta, GA

CREATING WEALTH

Whether you earn an additional $5,000 or $5,000,000 a year from the business of music, remember to always put a percentage of your earnings (money that you make) aside, preferably in a tax-sheltered account and invest your money in businesses that have nothing to do with the music industry. This is called diversification of your assets (money). In addition, **you want to always pay yourself first**, spend less money than you earn, carry little to no debt and keep accurate and complete records of the money you earn and spend. This will increase your chances for long-term wealth creation and retention. **Educate yourself about business and money; after all if you don't mind your business and money, someone else will.** To ensure you advance your own learning on saving, investing and creating wealth I have listed a few terms below that you should know.

- **401(k)**
- **Annuities**
- **Assets**
- **Asset Allocation**
- **Bonds (Corporate, Convertible & Government)**
- **CD (Certificate of Deposit)**
- **Checking Account**
- **Compounding Interest**
- **Debt to Income Ratio**
- **Diversification**
- **Dollar-Cost Averaging**
- **Earnings**
- **Equity**
- **Financial Freedom**
- **Index Funds**
- **Inflation**
- **Investment Portfolio**
- **IRA-Individual Retirement Account**
- **Keoghs**

- **Market Index**
- **Money-Market Accounts**
- **Money Market Mutual Funds**
- **NAV (Net Asset Value)**
- **No-Load Mutual Funds**
- **Passive Income**
- **Prospectus**
- **Real Estate**
- **Residual Income**
- **ROI (Return on Investment)**
- **Roth-IRA, SEP-IRA, Simple-IRA**
- **Savings Account**
- **Stocks**
- **Tax Sheltered Accounts**
- **Treasury Bills**

Educate yourself about investing and seek the advice of professionals who may help you verify your information. Publications that may help you become familiar with saving and investing your money are Black Enterprise, The Wall Street Journal, Kiplinger, Money, Smart Money, Barron's, Investor Business Daily, Financial Times, the Business Section of the Atlanta Journal Constitution and the Money Section of USA Today. For more information on saving, investing and making your money grow; visit the following websites.

- **www.bankrate.com**
- **www.blackenterprise.com**
- **www.fool.com**
- **www.indexfunds.com**
- **www.investoreducation.org**
- **www.jumpstartcoalition.org**
- **www.kiplinger.com**
- **www.marketwatch.com**
- **www.mfea.com**
- **www.money.com**
- **www.moneyopolis.org**
- **www.moringstar.com**
- **www.smatmoney.com**

- **www.tiaacref.com**
- **www.troweprice.com**
- **www.vanguard.com**

$$$$$$$$$$$$$$$$$$$$$$$$$$$$$$$$$

WEALTH BUILDING KIT

Save, Invest & Create Wealth

You Will Discover

- How to keep more money in your pocket
- How to make your money grow
- Simple budgeting techniques
- How to save, invest and create wealth
- How to buy a home with a low down payment
- Legally, protect your assets (money) from taxes
- How to use mutual funds to create wealth
- Plus get information on annuities, bonds, CDs (certificate of deposits), money-market mutual funds, retirement accounts i.e. 401(k)s, Keoghs, Roth-IRAs and SEP-IRAs, stocks, treasury notes, wills and trust.

The Wealth Building Kit retails for $19.95, however as a way of saying thank you for investing in the Atlanta Music Industry Connection Book, you may use the order form at the end of this chapter to order your Wealth Building Kit today for $9.95. The Wealth Building Kit takes 4 to 6 weeks for delivery.

Neither the author nor publisher offer investment or tax advice. The reader should always seek help from an investment and tax professional before making any investment decisions. The Wealth Building Kit is for information & educational purposes only.

$$$$$$$$$$$$$$$$$$$$$$$$$$$$$$$$

T-Shirts, Sweat Shirts, Jackets
Baby Tees, Polos
Mouse Pads
Tote Bags
& much
more...
Ask about
100 Custom
T-Shirts
for $4 ea
YOUR
LOGO
HERE
Screen Printing
& Embroidery
HOT4SHIRTS
770.409.0250
2500 Lawrenceville Hwy
Atlanta, GA 30033
HOT4SHIRTS.com
TM

MUSIC THERAPY 101 MEMBERSHIP

Annual subscription to the MIC (4X) yr	$ 4
Record Pool Directory (over 130)	$15
Atlanta's Music Industry Connection	$12
Two 40-Word Text Ads in the MIC Ezine	$40
One biz card Ad in the MIC Newspaper	$50
Savings on Music Therapy 101 Music Biz Conferences 10%	Min.
Split Sheet	$5.00
Total	$126.00
Membership	$125.95
DISCOUNT	$ 26.00
Your Membership Price	**$ 99.95**

Please complete the order-form at the end of this book to join the Music Therapy 101 Membership Program.

To get your name listed in the Music Industry Connection BOOK send your name, company name, physical mailing address, phone & fax number, website, email and the category you would like your company listed. Send your information to The MIC BOOK,
P.O. Box 52682, Atlanta, GA 30355 or kemetic0@yahoo.com.

ABOUT THE AUTHOR

JAWAR

Chief Visionary Officer of Music Therapy 101, a Music Business Conference since 1998, has given informative seminars in Atlanta, Los Angeles and Washington D.C. He created the workshop to identify and share vital information in a step-by-step process necessary for success and ultimate longevity in the music biz with aspiring artists and those willing to be involved in the music industry.

In 2002, JaWar created the MIC (Music Industry Connection) one of the few free all Music Business Publications that serves all genres of music. In just over a year the MIC tripled is circulation, doubled its' page count and increased its' subscription base. When your event demands practical, relevant, and useful information from an enthusiastic speaker who has legitimately "been there" by releasing the Dark Ages II & Paranormal Activity CDs on his independent record company Kemetic Records consider JaWar; he may be contacted at 800-963-0949, jawar@mt101.com or P.O. Box 52682, Atlanta, GA 30355, USA.

MAIL ORDER FORM

Please mail me the following music business items to help me achieve my goals & realize my potential. I have completed the attached order form and will include a check or money order for my total and mail it payable to:

MUSIC INDUSTRY CONNECTION, LLC
P.O. BOX 52682, Atlanta, GA 30355, USA

Name:		
Company Name:		
Mailing address:		
City:	State:	Zip:
Phone:	Fax:	
Email:		
Comments:		

www.mt101.com 800-963-0949

Item Description	PRICE Per Item	# Of Items	Total
Atlanta's Music Industry Connection E-Book on CD	$13.95		
Atlanta's Music Industry Connection Book	**$13.95**		
Record Pool (over 130) E-Directory on CD	**$13.95**		
Record Pool (over 130) Directory Print Version	$13.95		
Wealth Building Kit	**$ 9.95**		
One-year subscription to the MIC, four issues	$ 4.00		
One-year Music Therapy 101 Membership	$99.95		
SUBTOTAL	/////////		
Shipping & Handling Add $3.00	/////////		
GA residents add 7% sales tax.	/////////		
TOTAL	/////////		

MAIL ORDER FORM

Please mail me the following music business items to help me achieve my goals & realize my potential. I have completed the attached order form and will include a check or money order for my total and mail it payable to:

MUSIC INDUSTRY CONNECTION, LLC
P.O. BOX 52682, Atlanta, GA 30355, USA

Name:

Company Name:

Mailing address:

City: State: Zip:

Phone: Fax:

Email:

Comments:

www.mt101.com 800-963-0949

Item Description	PRICE Per Item	# Of Items	Total
Atlanta's Music Industry Connection E-Book on CD	$13.95		
Atlanta's Music Industry Connection Book	**$13.95**		
Record Pool (over 130) E-Directory on CD	**$13.95**		
Record Pool (over 130) Directory Print Version	$13.95		
Wealth Building Kit	**$ 9.95**		
One-year subscription to the MIC, four issues	$ 4.00		
One-year Music Therapy 101 Membership	$99.95		
SUBTOTAL	/////////		
Shipping & Handling Add $3.00	/////////		
GA residents add 7% sales tax.	/////////		
TOTAL	/////////